PREPARED & ARMED

TEAM SHOOTING TACTICS FOR HOME DEFENSE

JOSEPH TERRY

IR
Living Ready BOOKS
IOLA, WISCONSIN
www.LivingReadyOnline.com

CONTENTS

PART 4: OPERATING AS A FIRE TEAM

APPENDIX

Dedication

This book is fondly and respectfully dedicated to my father, George. TSgt, 32nd ID, WWII. CIB, Bronze Stars (5). Battles of: Buna-Gona, Sananada, Dobadura, Hollandia, and the invasion of Leyte. He refused a battlefield commission (skipping grade) direct to 1st Lt. because he would have to transfer out and leave his buddies in the outfit. The boys in the "Red Arrow" Division left their youth and blood fighting the Japanese in the rotting jungles of New Guinea and the Philippines defending our republic from invasion. Now, it's up to us to protect it from chaos. The sacrifice of the greatest generation deserves no less.

———————————

"Any man who is a man may not, in honor, submit to threats of violence. But many men who are not cowards are simply unprepared for the fact of human savagery. They have not thought about it (as incredible as this may appear to anyone who listens to the news) and they just do not know what to do. When they look into the face of depravity or violence they are astonished and confused."

—COL. JEFF COOPER

"Somebody who thinks there is good in all men ... has not met all men."

—LAW ENFORCEMENT PROVERB

PREFACE:
DISASTERS AND THE HUMAN CONDITION

During the more than twenty-seven years I've been involved with law enforcement, I have seen disasters bring out the best and worst in the human condition. Some people rise to the occasion and demonstrate remarkable heroism, self-sacrifice, and focused determination to survive. Others will rob, rape, and steal simply because, if unfettered by traditional law enforcement, they can.

Here is a dose of reality known to every street cop—cities and counties hire the absolute minimum number of officers and deputies necessary to handle the average pace of criminal activity. If some disruption, natural or man-caused, dramatically increases the number of felonies taking place, local law enforcement can be quickly overwhelmed. If neighboring departments are hit with the same disaster, mutual aid protocols collapse. The corrections system (prisons and jails) will also be overwhelmed and stop functioning. Expect mass escape of prisoners who will operate in well-organized looter gangs.

In the absence of traditional law enforcement services, responsible citizens must step into the breech to protect their neighborhoods from the looting that has now become commonplace in the wake of such disasters. This book is a sample protocol on how citizens can fill that breech ethically and effectively.

It has long been fashionable for the cultural elites to look down on the preparedness community as a bunch of knuckle draggers or collapse-fantasy addicts. This book is hardly evidence of a perverse hope that a disaster will occur. Like a fire extinguisher or a first aid kit, it is simply a prudent investment in case one does. The greatest emergency preparedness tool is a nimble brain, but the brain needs to be constantly fed with new ideas to function properly. It's not even important that you agree with all the ideas presented in this book; simply process them and find points that fit your application.

Your opinions may be quite different from mine on this topic, and that's fine. This book just gives you a chance to think about what you might be up against if you get a busy signal when you dial 911.

BUILDING AN EFFECTIVE, WELL-BALANCED FIRE TEAM

Although I strongly recommend you build a comprehensive personal library on all topics related to family disaster preparedness, I have excerpted what I believe to be the most relevant points from my own collection just in case you don't. I have drawn from more than forty published reference works cited in the bibliography, and they represent a wealth of knowledge to supplement my own particular experience. Each reference cited is worth a closer look, and in this age of internet shopping, they are only a click away.

Incidentally, you can have a comprehensive preparedness library in your pocket with an e-reader device, sustained by a crank radio with a charger adapter. Knowledge is power and e-readers can store a wealth of practical information in a small package.

While the thrust of this book is the advanced tactical use of defensive firearms, much of the content is secondary survival-related material, but is still important to know. It is sobering to remember that in the American Civil War, more casualties were caused by disease, post-operative infection, and poor sanitation than gunfire. In a prolonged social collapse or regional natural disaster, much of the American landscape could be thrust into such primitive conditions as the 1860s with a lack of clean water, proper sanitation and healthy food. Deprivation causes panic, and panic is the mood-state that drives the mob.

In an absence of traditional law enforcement services, local groups of responsible citizens can be forged into an effective defensive force (what I will refer to in this book as a "fire team") to deter mob aggression. Although the well-coordinated use of firearms is the foundation, it is only one facet of a complex survival task. (Guns are only tools after all.) One member of the fire team needs to be trained in health and wound management, one in communications, codes and navigation, and one in primitive living and outdoor survival skills. All of these areas are covered in this book in some detail because in coping with disaster, the devil will still be lurking in the details. It doesn't matter if you learn how to gunfight as a group if your members are flat on their backs with dysentery or dehydration.

And although understanding equipment is important, don't rush to the store just yet. (People often try to fix a problem by buying something.) Far better to think in the greatest detail possible about the unique challenges you, your family and your neighbors might face and then purchase your equipment.

The objective of this book is to help you project yourself into the harsh contingencies of self-reliance in considerable detail, with the hope that you will never need to actually confront them. The power comes from knowing that if you must, you could. No sane person looks forward to a gunfight, and we should all do everything feasible to avoid it. But if that horrible last resort is thrust upon us, we have only two choices; fight back or die. Prevailing in an armed encounter requires the mental willingness to confront the possibility and the discipline to prepare for it. If you are ready, read on.

ETHICAL CONSIDERATIONS

Some of my colleagues in law enforcement may shudder at the thought of sharing team gunfighting techniques with civilians. That's unfortunate because well-prepared citizens can be law enforcement's best friends and strongest allies. In the Old West, when the bank was robbed or the stage was held up and the town sheriff put out the posse call, regular folks dropped their hay forks and shop towels and grabbed their guns and rode with him. In the frontier days, keeping the peace wasn't a duty for "them," it was a duty for "us." On September 7, 1876, the notorious James/Younger gang of bank robbers was blown out of their saddles in Northfield, Minnesota, by angry townspeople who had their rifles handy. Lesson learned? Don't try to rip people off on the opening week of deer season!

And looking to civilians to help law enforcement is not just something from the history books. I shared some tactical training with an Alaska State Trooper who described flying his bush plane solo into small villages to deal with … whatever. "How far away is your cover?" I asked. "When I land," he said with a modest smile, "I'm always met by two or three locals who I know from past experience will back me up just fine."

The topics covered in this book are more complex, of course. Nobody wants tactical tips to end up in the wrong hands, but after much reflection I think they probably won't. I've helped process hundreds of prisoners into custody, and never, not once, included a book on their property inventory sheet or found one when we impounded their cars or tossed their apartments. Gangbangers and self-absorbed young sociopaths may be cunning, but they appear as a class, almost entirely illiterate.

None of this information requires a security clearance. These techniques are all described in the public domain and well demonstrated in the recent crop of special ops movies, some of which are quite good. And if a bad boy does happen to get his hands on this book, it would probably be a good idea for him to keep this in mind: If you think your crew can take on SWAT because of this information, think again. The "young guns" in black suits will clean your clock. I've watched them stand on the line and ping metal plates with their pistols from fifty yards just for kicks. From across the room, they can put three suppressed rounds into a target the size of a softball with a sound like a quiet fart in less than a second. From three-hundred yards out, they can put a sniper round through a triangle the size of your eyes and chin. In Dirty Harry's immortal words, "Do you feel lucky, punk?"

The bottom line is this: If you believe in the Second Amendment and even more important, the natural right to defense of self and family, "the people" should be not only be able to own guns but know how to use them effectively in coordinated defensive action. To deal with the probable consequences of low-probability events, they should know how to gunfight as a team.

DISCLAIMER

This book is designed to deal with the low-probability event of a prolonged regional elimination of traditional law enforcement and prosecutorial services. Such a disruption does not automatically preclude the possibility of subsequent criminal charges or civil liability based on the allegation of unjustified use of lethal force. Even if the situation clearly demands it, you may still be prosecuted or sued for your actions. In other words, the system that abandons you may come back to life and seek retribution because you had the audacity to defend yourself.

If a display of force and verbal orders to disperse do not suffice and you must take lives to protect your own and the dependents under your protection, I strongly recommend that you document the incident in writing as soon as possible, including; (a) date, time and location, (b) precise nature of the threat, (c) actions you took to try to avoid the threat ("display of arms and verbal admonition"), (d) why you felt you could not avoid the use of lethal force, and (e) printed names and signatures of adult witnesses. Bury one copy on site in a moisture-proof container and keep one copy with your other important records. If in subsequent actions your decisions were ever questioned, a professional-looking narrative post-action report could help counteract the verbal recollection of dubious characters.

INTRODUCTION:
WHY FIRE TEAMS?

The goal of this book is to help you protect your home. The fortified house is as American as baseball and apple pie. Long before the United Sates became a leading power in the world, a seemingly endless frontier beckoned the bold of Europe with free land and rich soil. "Farmsteads" and wagon tracks spread their tendrils into the wilderness. Hearty immigrant families claimed and tamed the land bearing their children along the way. It was a violent process as cultures clashed. Proud Iroquois, Huron, Cherokee and other earlier migrating peoples at first greeted the settlers warmly but soon learned the perils of European diseases, the greed of their land speculators, and the degradation of their alcohol.

The expansion of pioneer settlements beyond the coastal plain was one of almost constant desperate battles. As warnings of Indian predations spread, small groups of homesteaders would gather with their families at a central place, usually the largest and strongest cabin in the area, and prepare their resistance. A group of resolute men armed with rifles, working together in a well-fortified structure, could stand off an Indian raid. They could rotate sleep and guard duty, watch all angles of approach, and most important, cover each other during reloading so that a steady stream of accurate defensive gunfire could be maintained. They became, driven by dire necessity, a "fire team." One man in one cabin with one gun had no chance, and the price was often paid in the blood of his children.

Flash forward several centuries to the often dubious benefits of modern civilization and the idea of a fortified residence is making a comeback, especially with those who respect professional law enforcement but know only too well how fragile their infrastructure is. In case of prolonged social collapse or regional natural disaster, our reality could become the same as it was for our ancestors. No single shooter, no matter what his or her skill level, motivation, or quality of firearms, can defend a structure against a determined armed mob of looters. To think otherwise is delusional.

No modern city can feed itself. Cities rely on food supplies produced well outside their boundaries. It's been my observation that the average family has less than two weeks of food in reserve.

In the wake of recent natural disasters, it's not difficult to imagine everyday life being disrupted for more than two weeks. Even in the safest of times, society has a criminal element preying on the vulnerability of others. In the wake of disaster, these criminals will be even more emboldened. And as unrest grows among the general population, the longer the grid remains down, it's not hard to imagine food and water riots. Desperate people will do desperate things.

We hire law enforcement professionals to protect us, but then saddle them with rules so constricting that they must be warriors, social workers and civil rights attorneys simultaneously. We require cops to make life-or-death decisions in three-fifths of a second, and if they happen to get it wrong … we might just put them in jail. The next time you see a cop or deputy on the street, make deliberate eye contact and give them a smile and a friendly wave. On a hard and otherwise thankless day, that little gesture means more to us than you can possibly imagine.

The world of law enforcement has changed a lot since I joined it in 1983. Did you know that when a riot starts, it is now standard tactical doctrine for Watch Commanders to immediately pull all of their uniformed officers away from the affected area? Hard-core rioters can hold entire city blocks knowing very well that there will be little or no police intervention for hours. With a sprinkling of arson and random gunfire, rioters can hold large parts of any city for days. It takes that long for department brass to:

- call for mutual aid
- stage at a remote location
- check with the mayor about what force can be used, and
- quell the "unrest" under the harsh glare of the TV lights

If you happen to be an innocent store owner or lost tourist in the midst of that riot, tough. In the old days, the cop on the beat shot the first guy who refused to drop an armload of looted goods and guess what, everybody else went home empty handed. Hence the old saying in Texas, "One riot? One Ranger!"

If terrorists hack into the power grid and fry our generators, or we suffer a weather-related national crop failure, or an electromagnetic pulse (EMP) fries our electronics, or the computer-dependent finance system implodes, or the Yellowstone caldera blows, multiply overwhelmed law enforcement by ten thousand cities and you have a glimpse of the challenges facing your local cops. Any of these seemingly low-probability events has major implications for your neighborhood. The thin blue (or brown) line, as brave as it is, is very thin indeed, and expecting that the police or sheriff's deputies can protect your home and family in the face of a major natural disaster or prolonged social collapse is not realistic thinking.

The fantasy that one man with one gun can protect a structure from a gang of armed looters is just as wrongheaded as it was in the log cabin days. Why this myth is so persistent is open to conjecture. It might have something to do with the fact that the single-wronged-man-getting-retribution is so popular a theme on television and in the movies. Even if you see it a lot, it's still a fantasy. The reality is if a mob or gang comes after your home during a disaster, one looter will pin you down with gunfire while others force entry behind you and kill you without compunction. Your carefully stored survival supplies and dependent persons will then be theirs for pillage and amusement.

If desperate circumstances force my adult children and a few carefully selected friends to collect their families in the most defendable of their houses, they will have a lot more to think about than just staging extra food, water and medical gear. They will need to think about how they are going to defend those supplies against semi-organized gangs of armed looters, who through simple failure to plan or vicious criminal intent are likely to rampage if traditional law enforcement services collapse. As our ancestors eight generations ago learned, to successfully secure their supplies and dependent persons under their protection, they must also learn to fort up and gunfight as a group in closely coordinated action. I originally wrote this book for my kids. I pray they (and you) never need to use it.

There is a healthy balance possible between living with your head in the sand of denial and devoting your entire life to preparations for fending off your neighbors. That balance is simply to devote one day a month to preparing for the worst. That's all it takes to follow the recommendations in this book. One day a month is not a life of paranoia. It's all you need for a "fighting chance" to provide a bright future for your family through and beyond the worst that the power of nature or the folly of man can bestow. One day a month lets you still take all the time you need to smell the roses, to live a life of family activity, cultural pursuit, professional development, and volunteer community service.

PART 1

ASSEMBLING
YOUR FIRE TEAM

THE FUNCTION AND FORM
OF A CIVILIAN FIRE TEAM

Before you can successfully assemble your fire team and begin training, you must understand the purpose and makeup of a fire team. This chapter will explain the function and ideal composition of a fire team and describes the key attributes needed in fire team members.

For the purposes of this book, the definition of a civilian fire team is a group of three to five experienced shooters who are willing and able to use firearms in closely coordinated action to defend a fortified residence in case of the prolonged absence of traditional law enforcement services.

WHEN TO ACTIVATE A FIRE TEAM
The absence of conventional law enforcement resources is likely in any catastrophic natural disaster or prolonged social collapse. When 911 dispatch centers no longer function or indicate that response time to a specific request for service is impossible to predict, your fire team must communicate and decide if its time to activate. Fire team members should have the ability to make the activation call using independent communications capacity. As a rule, fire teams may elect to activate when certain predetermined circumstances occur, such as:

- regional interruption of the supply of water, power, or food
- evidence of wide-spread looting, assaults, rapes, or murders
- mass migrations of civilians
- collapse of the finance system
- nuclear or pandemic event

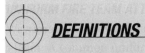

DEFINITIONS

Civilian Fire Team: A group of three to five experienced shooters who are willing and able to use firearms in closely coordinated action to defend a fortified residence in case of the prolonged absence of traditional law enforcement services.

Fortified Residence or Home: A structure that can provide shelter for several family units and is modified to provide enhanced resistance to mob attack. See chapter eight for more information on how to select and outfit a fortified residence.

Lethal Force: The effective use of firearms and/or field-expedient traps and explosive devices that may result in the death of armed looters.

THE PURPOSE OF A FIRE TEAM

Every law enforcement officer knows that gunfights are not won, they are survived. No sane person looks forward to an armed encounter. The purpose of a fire team is not to engage in a Wild-West style shoot-out with potential looters. The best-case scenario is one in which the fire team presents such an intimidating presence of force that the attackers are convinced to abandon their plans and leave the scene by their own choice and under their own power. In the law enforcement world, this is known as the achievement of "voluntary compliance." The best way to achieve voluntary compliance is to persuade looters that the risk their offensive behavior brings is not worth the reward of the stolen goods or rapes. Law enforcement refers to the capacity to project authority as "command presence." Command presence is the use of clear, forceful, verbal commands combined with the apparent willingness and capability to use whatever physical force is necessary if voluntary compliance is not achieved.

Command Presence

To be effective, a show-of-force deterrent must be backed up by the will and capacity to instantly go to guns. Only a fire team sufficiently trained and motivated to use deadly force can effectively project the will to use it. The criminal underclass in this country is very adept at sensing lack of willingness to resist. Effective deterrent is better than deadly force, but the threat of deadly force is only credible if the will and capacity to use it is clearly communicated to looters by:

- demonstration of arms
- physical posture
- clear and forceful verbal commands

When looters must be resisted, and voluntary compliance is still possible (i.e., no incoming rounds have been fired) the role of the fire team leader is to properly position the team and make clear verbal demands.

A demonstration of command presence through verbal instructions must include both a simple statement of what you want the subject(s) to do, and what will happen to them if they don't. Examples of command presence statements designed to achieve voluntary compliance are:

- "Stop now or we will fire on you!"
- "Turn away from me with your hands in the air or you will be shot!"
- "Drop your weapon or you will be shot!"
- "I have shooters you see and shooters you don't see. Back off or they will fire on you!"
- "Sniper! One warning shot low!"

Voluntary compliance on the part of the looters is dramatically improved if the fire team leader combines command presence with the implied threat of lethal force by more than one shooter. If circumstances allow, other shooters on the team should flank out to positions near cover but remain visible with weapons at the ready. Auxiliary shooters should also be visible. With the threat of lethal force from different directions, the credibility of the verbal commands becomes significantly magnified.

Spreading shooters to the right and left of the person making contact with the mob also provides security against a flanking movement by the looters. Team members have an important role as backup to the leader in an attempt to achieve voluntary compliance. For their own protection, however, they must be visible but within a step of cover.

Credible Alternatives to Lethal Force

Fire team members dedicated to a defensive use of coordinated gunfire do not shoot to kill—they shoot to eliminate the threat. In a broad social collapse scenario, if alternatives to lethal force are equally effective in convincing looters to voluntarily move on, that is vastly preferable to using gunfire. Such alternatives might include:

- visible show of force
- verbal intimidation or threat of force
- less than lethal force
- warning shots

The hoped-for objective of a well-trained fire team is to persuade looters to choose to go elsewhere through the aggressive display of arms and tactics. Effective nonlethal alternatives to achieve voluntary compliance are always preferable to the use of lethal force. However, if no alternative to lethal force is possible or appears effective, then aimed and suppressive fire should be directed against the threat until that threat is eliminated.

Effective non-lethal alternatives to achieve voluntary compliance are always preferable to the use of lethal force.

The Use of Lethal Force

Lethal force is the effective use of firearms and/or field-expedient traps and explosive devices that may result in the death of armed looters. However, the purpose of the use of firearms and other devices is not to cause death. The purpose of using lethal force is to eliminate the threat of grievous bodily injury (including rape) or death to members of the team or dependent persons under their protection.

In a prolonged survival situation, the protection of food, water, and medical supplies is also a clear moral justification for the use of lethal force if a reasonable person would conclude that the theft or destruction of those supplies would likely cause death to the people who are depending on them in a long-duration crisis environment.

Ask ... Tell ... Take

The taking of a human life, even under situations of clear self-defense can be a very traumatic experience for the shooter. To maintain combat effectiveness through what might be a prolonged situation of social unrest, every shooter on the team needs the emotional security of understanding and practicing the time-honored police strategy of, "Ask ... Tell ... Take." You first ask for compliance. If compliance is not achieved, you demand compliance. If compliance is still not achieved, you take whatever action the situation demands, including the precision application of gunfire, to protect yourself or persons or property under your care. Don't be so quick to go to guns if other alternatives are equally acceptable. *Guns should always be last-resort tools.*

Fire team tactics should be strictly limited to defensive applications. This restriction has positive psychological and practical implications. Most people outside the warrior culture (by which I mean street cops and elite military) are not psychologically prepared to take a human life. It is estimated that only 2 percent of active military and police can engage in prolonged close-range mortal combat without a debilitating psychological effect. When facing a lethal threat, even experienced cops can draw a breath, close their eyes, or freeze. Only in a survival situation in which effective resistance to armed looters is required to protect dependents and critical supplies of food, water, and medicine can the use of lethal force be justified. The context is the justification.

KEY ATTRIBUTES OF FIRE TEAM MEMBERS

Understanding the purpose of a fire team will help you understand the key attributes needed in fire team members. All potential fire team members must be able to legally possess and safely store weapons and ammunition sufficient to meet potential long-term defensive needs. See lists A and B in the appendix. Potential fire team members must also already be competent in the basic defensive use of the handgun, rifle, and shotgun. All of the information presented in this book is based on the presumption that the fire team members meet both of the aforementioned criteria.

A fire team member must have three essential qualities:
1. highly skilled in gun use
2. absolutely trustworthy to the other members of the team
3. a good listener and facilitator of others opinions

Fire team members must be so highly skilled in gun use and trust each other so much, that they can shoot behind each other's backs safely, effectively, and with absolute confidence. The key is *absolute confidence.* That means that a fire team member stationed on one side of a fortified residence will not leave his or her post because a fellow team member is engaging armed looters attacking from the opposite direction. He will concentrate fully on protecting his own area of responsibility because he assumes that his teammate will handle his own area of responsibility. This skill level can only be maintained with regular, scenario-based training for the entire team, and training exercises will be presented in this book to sustain that level of proficiency.

Only in a survival situation in which effective resistance to armed looters is required to protect dependents and critical supplies of food, water and medicine can the use of lethal force be justified.

HOW LARGE IS A FIRE TEAM?

In a civilian defensive application, the ideal size of fire team is between three and five skilled shooters. Three competent shooters represent the minimum number necessary to defend a fortified residence. Five is probably the maximum number of shooters who can be well coordinated by a designated leader. Each of the three shooters preforms a distinct role that requires special skills. These roles and skills are detailed in chapter nine.

You have two pools to choose from when choosing members of your fire team: friends or family. The most probable model for a fire team involves three male heads of households, but as aptly demonstrated by the citizen army of the State of Israel, certain women have the capacity to perform equal to any man in Close Quarter Battle (CQB) and should be granted equal opportunity to qualify for fire team status if they wish to participate at that level.

It is certainly possible that in some families, three to five skilled shooters could be found in the same family, in which case the family could stay in its own home and defend itself. That model may present other complications, however. If the head of the household cannot delegate authority smoothly to the family member with the most shooting expertise (because they prefer to maintain control and command), this does not bode well for the survivability of the family in a gunfight where hard decisions by the designated fire team leader must be obeyed instantly and without hesitation.

The three head-of-households model is especially functional if all three families have children in the fortified residence. The principal advantage of this type of fire team is that all three shooters will share a common need to protect their families, and their spouses will be able to cooperate skillfully and effectively in managing the retreat logistics given adequate forethought and preparation.

The fortified residence will house more than just the fire team members. It will also house members' families and anyone else selected to shelter in the fortified residence. In this book, I will refer to this larger collective group of fortified residents as a survival group. When you select members of your fire team, keep in mind that you are also selecting their family members as part of your survival group. It's essential that everyone in the survival group is able to get along and function with the best interests of the group in mind. Chapter two fully explains how to select members of a survival group.

TRAINING AS A FIRE TEAM

To put it as plainly as possible, only after the shooter can safely and consistently qualify on the target range, should any type of tactical firearms training begin. As you prepare to train keep, these two points in mind:

1. Do not practice fire team tactical techniques as a group with centerfire or rimfire ammunition unless you are under the immediate supervision of a qualified professional firearms instructor.
2. Do not practice fire team tactical techniques as a group without strict adherence to proper safety protocols and equipment.

Historically, training individuals on how to gunfight in small teams has been strictly limited to elite combat military units and law enforcement special weapons and tactics operators. Fire team training, even for those individuals, has been a relatively recent phenomenon. For the United States military, the serious academic study of small teams in contact with the enemy began in 1962 with President John Kennedy's support for the SEALS and Green Berets. SWAT (police; "special weapons and tactics") was first developed by the Los Angeles Police Department after a confused response to a neighborhood shoot-out with a heavily armed domestic terrorist group in 1974. Interestingly, most police departments did not even have SWAT teams until after the popular TV show *SWAT*, glamorized the capabilities of the LAPD unit. All over the country, cops watched that show and said, "That's cool! We gotta get some of that!" After much trial and error, the common core of SWAT operations became then and remains today:

- highly trained small teams of experienced shooters
- under clear tactical command
- simultaneously engaging multiple lethal threat targets with precision fire
- emerging from any position in a 360-degree threat zone
- using highly focused aggression

Fire team training is as close as a civilian can come to that experience. Advanced tactical training of this type must rest on the sound fundamentals of safe gun handing, and those techniques will also be presented in this book in some detail. It is important to remember, however, that individual firearms training, no matter how often or extensively it is practiced, is not fire team training. Effective individual firearms training with full power firearms is an indispensable foundation for team shooting and should always be encouraged, but unless the full team practices regularly in an area where targets can be safely engaged at various distances in any direction, they will not develop the necessary confidence in fellow team members to achieve fire team level proficiency.

Individual firearms training, no matter how often or extensively it is practiced, is not fire team training.

Civilian fire team training is based on the principals that:

- The threat zone surrounds the group at all times.
- The group will always be outnumbered and threats can appear from any direction at any time.
- Regardless of the location of other members of the group, any fire team member that has a shot should take the shot.

Training small teams to engage multiple targets at varied angles with aimed fire is very different from typical firearms training. It is inherently dangerous. Basic firearms training for almost all civilian and most law enforcement shooters follows the linear training model on a flat range. Students stand on a designated firing line an equal distance from stationary targets placed directly to their fronts and fire. Although most experienced police firearms instructors agree that linear training on a flat range does not prepare shooters well for the dynamic chaos of a gunfight, it is the cheapest way to train the most people in the shortest possible time, and we have been stuck with it.

For law enforcement administrators and private shoot-school insurance providers, the liability risk of being sued for "unsafe training practices" simply outweighs the average student's need for training to shoot in a group. The sorry result is that most cops, the majority of military service persons, and virtually all civilians have never experienced live-fire, 360-degree threat management training. (Fortunately, I have a solution to that problem later on in this book.)

The coordination of force also involves advanced tactical skills designed to focus maximum effective gunfire on any lethal threat while minimizing the risk of the engagement to members of the team. Although these will be amplified later, four basic tactics must be mastered to achieve "coordinated use of force:"

1. cover and concealment
2. tactical maneuver
3. overlapping fields of fire
4. flanking and enfilade fire

Practically speaking, unless the full team drills together frequently enough to convert perishable skills to muscle memory, they will not be effective in combat. If they are not well trained, they cannot project an image of effective deterrent to lethal force. To be brutally blunt, three competent shooters could persuade twenty looters to back off only if they knew they could put them down if they had to.

2 SELECTING MEMBERS FOR A FIRE TEAM AND SURVIVAL GROUP

While the fire team itself is composed of three to five shooters, this team will be a part of and responsible for defending a larger survival group. Most likely, this survival group will consist of the fire team's family members. This chapter will help you assemble a survival group that contains a fire team.

HOW TO APPROACH POTENTIAL SURVIVAL GROUP MEMBERS

Warning! In your discussions with potential survival group members, don't be too aggressive in your stories about impending disaster. The easiest way to turn off good potential allies is to sound alarmist. Better than sounding paranoid with friends is to start off with a very simple, common sense premise:

Because we are already friends, let's agree to support each other in case of a (pick the one that is the most likely localized risk):

- *hurricane*
- *tornado*
- *blizzard*
- *earthquake*
- *flood*

Each home will be open as a "safe house" for each other's kids. We all agree to store extra:

- *food*
- *water*
- *medical supplies*

And regularly discuss how we might cooperate in an emergency.

Your survival group will need to designate leaders for all of the important survival categories including:

- food supplies and cooking
- medical supplies and care
- hardening the residence
- security
- child care and support
- communications

Obviously, under a forting-up scenario, other members of the survival group will help each leader execute the duties in each category. Keep repeating the motto, "we're all in this together," and make every aspect important. In the case of security, I recommend taking a more subtle approach that does not imply that readiness is "all about guns."

In my opinion, the best way to approach comprehensive readiness for disaster is to refer to armed defense as a "worst-case" only response. When discussing preparedness with all the adults in the survival group, don't treat guns as any more relevant than any other important aspect of planning. As tasks are distributed based on areas of competence or interest, simply include "security" as a factor that requires training and specialized equipment.

CHAIN OF COMMAND IN A SURVIVAL GROUP

It very important that the fire team and especially the leader of the fire team not become the presumptive leader of the entire fortified home. The best way to govern the survival group is through democratic process that involves all

 DEFINITIONS

Survival Group: A group of individuals committed to providing mutual aid in the event of a disaster. This group prepares together *ahead* of time by gathering supplies and creating clear action plans so they are ready when a crisis hits. Groups typically are made up of a number of nuclear families (i.e., parents and minor children) that may or may not be related (i.e., adult siblings who each have their own nuclear family). These groups are also known as readiness groups or preparedness groups, but for clarity, this book will refer to them as survival groups.

Line-Abreast Formation: A formation in which a group of shooters moves perpendicular to their objective.

adult members as equally important in the endeavor. As in all good organizations, communication is the key.

Many students of U.S. history think the best example of a functional democracy were New-England-style town meetings where every adult had an equal voice and an equal vote in how the town was going to be run. If a citizen disagreed with the majority view, the citizen still complied with the majority out of respect for the common good. When you think about the recruitment of members for your survival group, think about whether those prospects have the capacity to defer to the common good. Think about whether you do, too.

Maintaining a multi-family survival group over a considerable duration of time will have many challenges. Although the armed defense of that group will require "combat-style" leadership (defined in chapter nine), the day-to-day administration of that group will also be important and may require different skills entirely.

When the group comes in contact with potential or actual looters, the tactical authority of the fire team leader (who I refer to as *Point*) must be primary. *Tactical commands must be instantly given and instantly obeyed.* The survival group may delegate administrative leadership to the most qualified (and diplomatic) member of the group. The same person does not need to fill both the role of *Point* and administrative leader. If both the tactical leader and the administrative coordinator can lead by example and encourage the engagement of all members in important decisions, the "intangibles" should be well-managed.

SURVIVAL GROUP MEETINGS

The survival group should have regular meetings that are well regulated for time yet provide ample opportunity for group input on all important decisions. Avoid getting hung up on meeting protocol, but make sure that clear decisions are made, and the results are written down. Most people who have professional jobs are familiar with minutes and agendas. Use them, but don't go overboard with meeting rules and regulations. Follow this process:

- Call for votes on all important issues and ask for "all in favor?" (Simple majority rules.)
- Summarize each issue in one sentence in the minutes.
- Make a note in the minutes when an issue is passed.

Using this simple protocol, the responsibility of running the meeting can be rotated as can the responsibility of recorder. Keep the meeting notes and results in a three-ring binder. This record allows any member of the survival group to go back and review the discussions and the decisions. A suggestion

Camping together is a good way to test compatibility in survival group.

box is another good tool for group meetings. Some members may be introverts and less willing to speak up at meetings than the more assertive members. Agenda items can be put in the suggestion box anonymously, providing a vent for the opinions of the less-assertive but equally important members.

TESTING AND BUILDING A SURVIVAL GROUP

A critical element in building the fire team is compatibility of values. Obviously, fire team members will be connected by an interest in guns and shooting. But if team members' family values are at odds, the fire team likely won't be able to effectively engage in a well-coordinated gunfire or, better, present to looters a credible threat that will deter any shots from being fired in the first place.

To test compatibility under field conditions, I recommend that the families that might be forged into a survival group go camping together. Functioning without the traditional conveniences of home assesses initial camping patience, adaptability, and the capacity to share the workload. It's a great way to "test the water" in a safe, controlled environment.

This trip doesn't need to be a trek into the backwoods with no "luxuries," especially if some of the group members aren't experienced campers. Camping has come a long way since my wife and I took our toddlers with us backpacking to primitive locations in the High Sierra. Many people would respond better to the comparative luxury of a motor home or car-camping getaway to ease into the camping tradition. Most metropolitan areas have vendors that rent tent trailers, quite an inexpensive way to stay off the ground and bug-free. Even if the first group campfire is accompanied by the nearby hum of generators, the point is to get the families that are the candidates for your preparedness group out into the woods to test their ability to get along under new circumstances without friction. Forting up in a single structure (the core strategy of resistance to armed mobs) will be trying under the best of circumstances. Nudge up to the experience with group outings under progressively more primitive circumstances. Even group day hikes with a lunch rest stop are a great way to build unit cohesion. When you get outdoors, the whiners and shirkers will quickly identify themselves.

Preparing Your Own Family

As you start to develop a larger survival group, also work within your own family to make flexibility in living circumstances a regular part of life. Backpacking remains, in my opinion, the very best way to test a family's disaster coping skills including the ability to pack efficiently and keep calm nerves when the inevitable wild things go "bump" in the night. If you're backpacking in public lands that permit recreational shooting, bring along your guns and have some very carefully supervised age-appropriate training for all family members who wish it. Remember, .22's are quiet and fun, and don't push it. Shooting together will also get your family members used to seeing a pistol on your belt.

TEAM BUILDING FOR FIRE TEAM MEMBERS

After the families in your potential survival group have shown they are compatible, the same "field trip" technique can be used to develop the fire team that will defend the survival group. One of the best available training opportunities is to take the fire team on a guided hunt. With the explosion of wild pigs throughout most of the United States, guided pig hunts are available to every team that is sufficiently motivated to take the challenge. Research high quality guided hunt services in your area that offer a tactical-style hunting option. Tactical-style hunting means your group will move quietly through cover in a line-abreast formation to find the pigs rather than sitting in a lawn chair waiting for them to come to bait. Check to see if hunting pigs with a .223 is legal in your area and use your AR. While you are at it, you can even practice the communication techniques described in chapter eleven.

Stalking and killing a wild pig and harvesting the meat is a good test of the shooter's willingness to pull the trigger on a live target while developing some foraging skills. (The meat tastes great, when properly prepared, which is a nice bonus.) The field dressing and butchering process is just like taking a deer and is explained in detail online at livingreadyonline.com.

Survival Group Members as Auxiliary Fire Team Members

All responsible survival group members above the age of twelve, or so, might need to become auxiliary members of the group's defensive force. Under attack, they must either contribute directly to the defense or, at the very least, take cover and not disrupt the defender's concentration on the threat(s). Auxiliary members can make a significant contribution to that defense by delivering area saturation or suppressive fire, reloading magazines, or (positioned carefully behind cover) acting as spotters.

Although the relatively benign aspects of preparedness are not controversial (it's hard to find moral complications with canning carrots), some potential members of the survival group may either openly or through passive resistance balk at the notion of lethal-force capability. Many people who were raised with middle- or upper-class sensibilities and experiences are trained to avoid violence of any kind regardless of the provocation, and many have never even witnessed violence. I have nothing but respect for adults who are dedicated to pacifism as a way of life. The problem comes in the imposition of those values on children who may also be victims of mob violence. That cultural bias toward passivity cannot be overcome with harsh commands or a berating attitude. Interestingly, a cultural evolution in law enforcement offers a distinct parallel.

I've seen a lot of changes in how departments recruit and promote their officers over the last thirty years. In the 1980s the emphasis was still on "BTS" (big, tough and smart). Most recruits were military vets or buffed-up jocks with letters in tough contact sports. They had been hit plenty of times and they knew how to hit back. Virtually all were white males. As public demographics changed, recruitment and promotion patterns were opened up to reflect the communities the departments served. Though there were some rough spots, this change has been a good thing. One of the byproducts of this venting of testosterone was that we had to teach a lot of rookie cops (male and female) who had never held a gun or been in a fist fight how to defend themselves and their brother and sister officers and deputies on the dark and dangerous streets.

Tasers and OC spray became standard carry on every officer's duty belt, and now, when used effectively, allow smaller-stature officers to drop a burly suspect without having to grapple with or shoot them. Today, the ability to be an effective street cop is primarily determined by how quickly you respond to a threat and go to aggressive intervention with your tools, rather than how big and tough you look.

However, even with good tools, police departments know you can't get a rookie cop quickly into action with harsh commands or a berating attitude.

Most rookies learn on the job because of the universal motivator of human behavior—the law of necessity. It doesn't take long before the young officer or deputy is confronted with grisly examples of abject human depravity. During their probationary year, they learn the proper and timely use of force, or they are "encouraged" by their peers to seek employment elsewhere.

Your survival group members are no different from today's more diverse generation of law enforcement rookies. Although the survival group may be led by somebody with a keen eye on the risks and lots of trigger time, chances are very good that your group must adjust its recruitment and training protocols to include members who have no special interest in guns as a hobby or any comprehension of how startling it is to look into the eyes of somebody who, given half a chance, would kill you in a heartbeat.

I can't overemphasize, it's a serious mistake to try to use grisly stories of mob violence to scare reluctant members of the survival group into becoming fire team shooters. The probability of a regional or national disaster so profound as to suspend law enforcement services for an extended period still remains relatively low. Thankfully, most people in most short-duration disruptions will never need to use guns.

If members of the survival group who are not on the fire team are not interested in guns, don't force them to go to the range. Simply purchase and store firearms for their potential use that are, first, easy to shoot, and second, relatively potent. Good examples of easy-to-shoot and relatively potent guns are the classic GI M1 carbine and the new and excellent Mossberg 20 ga, semiauto combat shotgun. Under exigent circumstances, the training time for auxiliary fire team members might be short, but the law of necessity will kick in. Range days during the preparation phase should be "optional only." If a couple of the guys and gals and one of the older kids come back from the range abuzz with how much fun it was (and if you run it using the tips in chapter three they will) more will want to go the next time.

SUMMARY

No matter what the composition of the fire team, every member should read and understand this manual and meet every training criteria (see chapter four) to be considered a fire team member. A group of shooters can call itself a fire team, and expect the tactical benefits of one, only though the effective coordination of force, which comes out of participating in many, many training events together. Friends and family members are only *candidates* for fire team membership until they can demonstrate the skill level necessary to qualify for the slot. When in doubt, broaden your search.

TRAINING EXERCISES

1. Identify candidates for your fire team.
2. Purchase additional copies of this book and distribute them as training manuals.
3. Have a general discussion about disaster preparedness.

Objective: Establish your team.

Advanced Exercise: Take a day-long hike with a picnic stop.

Advanced Exercise Objective: Test patience, endurance, compatibility and team spirit.

3   BASIC GUN-HANDLING SKILLS

Although this book presumes that the reader is already competent in the basic skills of gun handling, it is certainly possible that an otherwise qualified person who is a new shooter might need to be integrated into the fire team. The purpose of this chapter is to outline a basic training protocol that the team leader can use to prepare a novice shooter for such inclusion.

UNDERSTANDING THE GUN

Assuming that the new shooter is equipped with a firearm that fits him or her properly (more on this later) and comports with the team unit standard, the most important principle in firearms training is don't rush it! In more than forty years of launching new shooters, I have learned that the most important training happens before you ever get to the range. I recommend you follow this home exercise whenever you help train a new shooter. This exercise is also helpful for a more experienced shooter to use whenever he or she gets a new gun.

1. Demonstrate how to show that the gun is empty of all ammunition. (Check it twice.)
2. Field strip the gun for the student by removing the action and magazine (if detachable), as you would if you were going to clean the gun. Do NOT disassemble the gun further at this point.
3. Explain how the parts groups interact to make the gun feed and fire.
4. Put the gun back together for the student.
5. Assist the student in field stripping the gun.
6. Prompt the student to "fill in the blanks" with key words as you explain the function of the parts groups.

7. Put the gun back together for the student.
8. Have the student field strip the gun themselves with your coaching.
9. Have them explain the function of the parts groups with minimum coaching.
10. Assist them in putting the gun back together.
11. When you think they are ready, have them replicate the entire process of field stripping, explanation, and reassembly while blindfolded.

The ability to field strip a gun without looking at it is a tremendous confidence booster for the student. One of the most common problems in efficient and safe gun operation occurs when the student does not understand the basic functioning of the gun. Many rookie cops I've trained with the pump-action shotgun had problems with "short-shucking" until we took the guns apart and demonstrated how retracting the forend to the full extent of its travel was necessary to chamber a round. ("Short-shucking" is slang for failure to fully cycle the action so that the carrier can lift a loaded shell and lock it into the breech. This is cured by teaching the student to push both hands together in a squeezing motion to insure full cycling.) Other cops had problems "limp-wristing" the semi-auto pistol until we demonstrated how the action worked and why it required a very firm grip on the gun to ensure reliable cycling. ("Limp-wristing" causes the action of the slide to be buffered by a weak hold on the pistol causing failures to feed.) These were otherwise sharp young officers. Don't think these problems represent lack of determination—just lack of understanding. To avoid these problems prior to each range session, have your student replicate the field stripping and basic functional explanation. (At the public range, leave the blindfold at home if you want to remain popular with the range master.)

GUN SAFETY

Before you ever get to the gun range, give your student plenty of time to learn safe gun-handing skills. Public ranges can be noisy, somewhat intimidating places for new shooters, and it's not always easy for the student to concentrate. At home, carefully demonstrate the following safety rules:

- Muzzle safe at all times.
- Mechanical safety "on" unless the gun is aimed at a specific target.
- Trigger finger indexed on the frame of the gun until it is aimed at a specific target.

I also teach all of my students, as simple matter of common courtesy, to never pass a gun to another person without opening the action and showing them it is empty. When you demonstrate unfailing attention to these safety habits, the new shooter will respect the habits because they respect you. (If you don't always demonstrate these habits, the new shooter is placing his trust in the wrong person.) So pick up the gun and check that it is empty, demonstrate the safety rules, open the action, show your student it is empty, pass the gun to him, and have him demonstrate the safety rules back to you.

Don't wait to do this at the range! Tell them the first lesson is always at home.

PRACTICAL ACCURACY

It's also quite easy to get the new shooter familiar with the principles of combat accuracy (the ability to put a projectile where you want it to go in the shortest possible time) with practice at home. Other books cover the basic elements of shooting proficiency in great detail (see *Police Handgun Manual* and *Police Shotgun Manual* by Bill Clede and *The Tactical AR-15* by Dave M. Lauck and Paul W. Hantke.) Suffice it here to simply mention them as:

- stance
- grip
- sight picture
- trigger press

Stance

One of the tricks I use with all shooters I train is to get them to present the gun from what I call a "fighting stance." Standing at ease, I ask them, "If I were to try to assault you right now, how would you prepare to resist me?" If you are lucky and they have some martial arts training or are athletic and intuitive, they will go into a natural defensive stance with:

- feet spread slightly more apart than shoulder width
- stepping into the threat with the weak side foot so that the feet are at a 45-degree angle to the threat
- knees slightly bent
- weight forward
- head upright
- arms up and forward in a good defensive posture

This is just like the position you want them to shoot from!

Another exercise you can use at home to demonstrate a good combat shooting stance is to have them stand facing you, flat footed, feet close together with their arms at their sides. Place your hand flat against their breastbone and give them a firm push (ask your female trainees permission first). This will almost certainly make them stagger back a couple of paces. Then you assume a

Remember, knees bent slightly and feet staggered and well apart make a solid and nimble shooting stance.

solid shooting stance and have them try to give you the same push. Although you may rock back a bit, unless they are a linebacker, your feet should remain properly placed. (If they are a linebacker, you can delete this exercise!) This is a very visceral way to explain the importance of a good shooting stance, and a good shooting stance is the foundation of all combat accuracy.

Maintaining a Good Stance: If your student's stance degenerates over time, another good training tool is to have him face you (without the gun) and use his strong-side foot to try to deliver a good front snap kick against your extended palm held waist high. If he is launching a good kick, his weak-side foot (the one in front) will remain planted, and he can return to a balanced stance after the kick. If he makes his kick and has to stumble around afterward, it usually means his stance is too "bladed" (feet in line with the threat and not spaced well apart at an angle to the threat). Correct this with demonstrations and repetitions until he can do the kick perfectly, then have him do the kick with an empty gun in low-ready shooting position. This, incidentally, is excellent preparation for shooting on the move, which will be a vital part of advanced fire team training. Remember, knees bent slightly and feet staggered and well apart make a solid *and* nimble shooting stance.

Grip

Once the new shooter assumes a solid shooting stance (or can be placed into one) it is time to address her grip on the gun. A proper grip is a critical foundation for practical accuracy, and a good grip is possible only if the gun fits the shooter. Here are some practical tips on how to find a good "fit." On a pistol or revolver, have the shooter hold out her strong-side hand with the thumb and index finger spread in a "V" shape as wide as is comfortable. Place the handgun into her hand with the web of her hand as high against the backstrap as possible with the line of the bore (the inside of the gun's barrel) in a direct line with the ulna bone (the large one) of the forearm. (The "backstrap" is a generic term for the rear of the grip of the handgun.) Check to see if this hold allows the shooter to place the pad of the first joint of the trigger finger comfortably on the trigger without having to shift her hand position on the grips.

To summarize, check the following to determine if the handgun fits the shooter:

- The web of the strong-side hand is high on the backstrap of the gun.
- The axis of the bore is in line with the shooter's ulna bone (the larger forearm bone).
- The pad of the trigger finger fits comfortably on the trigger.

For the defensive carbine or other long gun, the key to a good fit is to test what is called the "length of pull." This is the distance between the butt plate of the stock and the trigger. The best way to test the length of pull is to instruct the student to hold his strong-side arm out straight from his shoulder and then raise his forearm 90 degrees to the horizontal with his index (trigger) finger pointed straight up. The instructor then demonstrates the gun is empty and places it so that the butt stock rests in the crook of the student's elbow. If, from this position, the pad of the trigger finger can comfortably rest on the trigger, the length of pull is correct. This will correspond well to the ease the shooter will have in mounting the gun against his shoulder and finding the trigger.

If the length of pull is too long, the gun will not fit the shooter properly and subsequent training will be a challenge. If the length of pull is too short, the gun can be mounted and fired but the position will be awkward. The eye will tend to crowd the sights, and accuracy will suffer, especially on quick shots. Note: The ability to easily adjust the length of pull on the AR with an adjustable stock is another reason why this gun has become so popular.

Sight Picture

The ability to maintain a good sight picture is probably the single most important factor in the shooter's capacity to neutralize a lethal threat. You can have

When sighting with a handgun or rifle with iron sights, the focal point must be the front sight post or blade.

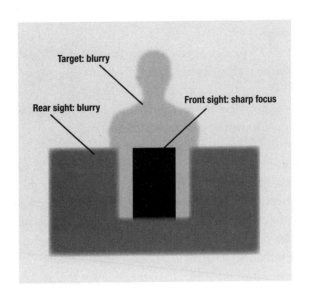

Target: blurry

Rear sight: blurry

Front sight: sharp focus

an awkward stance, a so-so trigger press, and a marginal grip, but if you have a good sight picture on the threat, you will probably put your adversary down. Conversely, you can be great in every other aspect of practical pistol shooting, but if your focus shifts from the front sight to the threat, you will probably miss. The physics are simple. An infinitesimal variation in the space between the rear sight notch and the front sight blade is magnified a thousand times in a fighting distance as small as fifteen feet.

A proper sight picture is much easier for a new student to master on a tactical carbine or battle rifle with electronic or telescopic sight because these guns have but a single reference point. A combat shotgun compensates in pellet spread for errors in the use of its typically crude sights. But with a handgun or rifle with iron sights, it takes a great deal of discipline to learn to use the sights properly. I have found that a simple visual aid can be a great help.

As the illustration shows, the focal point must be the front sight post or blade. The target should be described as a "general shape" against which the crystal clear front sight is placed. At the range, when the shooter is on target and using a gun with iron sites, keep repeating to the shooter, "Focus on the front sight. Focus on the front sight. Focus on the front sight."

Trigger Press

In the old days, firearms instructors used to describe activating the trigger as a "squeeze." The action really isn't a squeeze, because a squeeze implies moving opposing forces together, and in the case of a handgun, those opposing forces would be the thumb and trigger finger moving together in a pinching motion. Most instructors now refer to trigger activation as a "press" because only the trigger finger should move. The remaining structures of the hand(s) holding the gun should be dedicated to keeping the gun as still as possible. Only the trigger finger moves in a straight-to-the-rear, smooth and steady "press" until the sear is released and the gun fires.

One at-home exercise stands above all others in helping the student learn good trigger manners, and that exercise is "dry firing." *Dry firing* is a term that describes practicing pulling the trigger with the gun empty. After confirming (and demonstrating) that the gun is empty, put the new shooter in a good shooting stance and proper grip and have her aim at a specified target in the room in which you are training. Cock the action of the gun and have her practice her trigger press. After several replications, put a penny on the frame of the gun and try the trigger press again. If the shooter can consistently press the trigger without dropping the penny from the gun, she has good trigger management.

LIVE FIRE SESSIONS

You can then take the student to a safe place to shoot after the student is familiar enough with the gun that he can:

- field strip the gun
- explain the gun's functioning
- describe and demonstrate the three gun safety rules
- describe and demonstrate a good grip on the gun and solid shooting stance
- explain and demonstrate a good trigger press

I have had the best results with starting new students shooting at targets at the closest practical distance. At a public range, this distance is usually fifteen yards, and that's unfortunate. If you can find a place where you can shoot at five yards, that is much better for you and the student. It is critically important that the new shooter feel that the shooter is running the gun rather than the gun running the shooter. If her first shots hit the paper, it will immediately reinforce a sense of competence. Even if you tell the shooter, "We are not interested in hits at this point," the shooter's ego won't believe it, so make the distance short and use the blank side of the target sheet with a clear central aim point. Praise the shooter for any hits on the paper.

Make sure that the shooter (and you) have proper eye and ear protection. Keep your range time short and watch very carefully for fatigue. If you have a .22 "clone," you can usually get at least 150 rounds out of the shooter before he begins to tire. On a full-power gun, the first range session may be no more than twenty rounds. Don't try to do too much in one day at the range. If the shooter is comfortable, he will learn. If he's uncomfortable or tired, he won't learn.

Watch for these telltale signs that the shooter is fatigued:

- The shooter involuntarily blinks at the instant of discharge.
- The shooter pushes against the recoil of the weapon and the muzzle dips at each shot.
- The shooter forgets basic safety rules or good grip.

When this happens, it's time to end the live fire session (the longer you push the shooter at the range, the harder it will be to correct the problems), but I have learned the tremendous psychological importance of *always having the shooter finish a range session on a positive note.* Put the shooter five yards from a target and instruct him to fire two shots at the aim point as quickly as he can do so smoothly and with a good sight picture. When he puts two rounds in a space the size of a paper plate, give him a hearty handshake or shoulder squeeze and tell him, "I'm proud of you. You can defend yourself with that shooting any time you need to." Leaving the range on such a positive note will reinforce a positive attitude toward training and enhance the shooter's growing confidence in his ability to defend himself.

COVERT TRAINING

In a final note on basic firearms training, it is important to address the contingency of having to train a shooter during a system collapse that precludes the normal range orientation on how the gun functions (e.g., after your survival group has already assembled at your fortified residence). Firearms training makes noise, and noise discloses location. A new shooter can practice the loading, chambering, and unloading sequence using inert cartridges. Inert ("unable to explode") cartridges can be purchased for the most common calibers of 9mm., .38/.357, .223, and .308 and should be stocked at the fortified residence well in advance of a disaster. Inert cartridges are also easily made from loaded cartridges or fired brass following these steps:

1. Pull the bullet from the cartridge.
2. Dump the powder.
3. Explode the primer with a hammer and nail.
4. Fill the cartridge with sand. (This simulates the weight of the powder.)
5. Replace the projectile. (Use a wood plug or the original projectile.)
6. Paint or mark the inert cartridge red to distinguish it from live rounds.

Shooter orientation with a new firearm should always begin with slow repetition of:

1. Confirm empty.
2. Combat load.
3. Make safe.
4. Unload.
5. Confirm empty.

Doing this quietly and safely under close supervision is considerably easier with inert cartridges.

 ## TRAINING EXERCISE

For New Shooters
1. Identify a competent instructor.
2. Ask him to teach you basic gun handling techniques using the steps on pages 31–34.
3. Get sufficient range training to meet the performance criteria on pages 40–41.

Objective: To meet minimum fire team weapons proficiency standard

For Advanced Shooters: Train a friend or family member using the protocol in this chapter.

Objective: Hone your skills as an instructor

4 ADVANCED FIREARM SKILLS

If you are thinking about developing a fire team to cope with a possible collapse of traditional law enforcement services, you will be joining the elite ranks of combat military, fire and rescue, and law enforcement (who just happen to be about 2 percent of the American population). It's a commitment that is hard earned, often thankless, and always carries risks. And one of the most significant of those risks is accidental harm from other members of your own fire team in the chaos of the fight—what we in law enforcement call "blue on blue." (There is no such thing as "friendly" fire.)

To prevent the risk of this accidental harm, it is essential that each member of your fire team has demonstrated a mastery of the advanced firearms skills outlined in this chapter. The three techniques presented here should greatly reduce the risk team members pose to each other when they are facing a 360-degree threat zone.

QUALIFICATIONS FOR FIRE TEAM TRAINING

If you aspire to a fire team proficiency level, you must begin with a baseline level of shooting skill. Baseline ability doesn't mean you are qualified to fight as a fire team—only that you are qualified to be trained in fire team tactics. To meet the criteria for fire team training, each member of the fire team in training should be able to easily replicate the following exercise with every firearm he or she carries for defensive purposes:

- Pick up the gun and visually (and/or by feel) confirm that it is unloaded, keeping the muzzle safe at all times.
- Combat load the gun (full magazine and round in chamber) and "make safe."

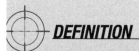

DEFINITION

"Sweeping" (also called "Painting"): Allowing the muzzle of your gun to pass across the body of another fire team member who is down range from you.

- Holster the handgun without looking at the holster and/or properly sling the carbine or rifle.
- On command, step into a strong shooting position and present the handgun or shoulder the long gun in a "low ready" position.
- On command, engage multiple targets at various distances and at various angles quickly and smoothly with two center-mass hits per target.
- On command, transition to kneeling and prone positions, and continue to engage multiple targets.
- On command, reload while running to a designated cover position without looking at the gun, magazines, or magazine holders.
- Smoothly clear failures to feed and get back into action quickly.
- Field strip, clean, and reassemble the gun without assistance.
- Pass the gun safely to the instructor for cleaning inspection, demonstrating it to be empty.

Practice this drill regularly so the actions become muscle memory.

CONDITIONING TO OVERCOME ADRENALINE "RUSH"

Humans are prisoners of their physiology. Under the catastrophic chaos of a gunfight, the body will be flushed with adrenaline (the "flight-or-fight" hormone). Veterans of gunfights report a similar set of automatic responses. Although physical strength is magnified, vision tends to tunnel in on the threat, fine motor skills are degraded, the passage of time seems to slow, and the risk of sympathetic muscle response dramatically increases. Unfortunately, you can never overcome the effect of adrenaline. You can only manage and mitigate its effect with frequent replications of the exercise described above.

Sympathetic Muscle Response

Most police firearms instructors believe that sympathetic muscle response is likely the leading cause of unintended discharges of a firearm by a police officer. Sympathetic muscle response occurs when the shooter with a hot weapon (round chambered and safety "off") is startled or must deal with the threat by taking aggressive physical action such as:

- tripping over an obstacle
- ducking a near miss
- jumping
- dropping to the ground
- blocking a strike

Sympathetic muscle response causes not just the muscle groups directly related to the physical action to tense dramatically but all muscle groups to tighten, including the fingers of the hands. In other words, the fingers (including the trigger finger) tighten "in sympathy" with the major muscle groups that respond to threat stimuli. This is the brain's natural physiological reaction to an urgent threat. The problem comes when the trigger finger involuntarily jerks the trigger sending a round in a direction that might cause more harm than good. Because of the inherent risk of fire team operations, the gun handling safety practices presented in this chapter must be deeply ingrained in all team members.

SAFETY TECHNIQUES FOR DOWNRANGE THREATS

Remember that a 360-degree threat environment means that fire team shooters may need to engage threats with precision gunfire even if other members of the team are between them and the threat. The reason for this is that although each member of the fire team has an assigned threat zone, the member of the team may not see every threat in that zone. Other members of the team must be able to shoot beyond the assigned fire team member to neutralize that threat without endangering the fellow team member. Another reason team members may need to shoot between a team member and threat is if one member of the team is in "overwatch" role and must engage threats approaching the team from any direction including directly beyond team members. To manage this downrange risk, fire team members must master these three weapons manipulation techniques to the point of muscle memory:

Technique 1: Trigger finger indexed along the frame of the gun until the gun is on target.

Technique 2: Muzzle safe at all times until the gun is on target.

Technique 3: Mechanical safety engaged until the gun is on target, and immediately reengaged after shooting.

Using all three of these techniques effectively and simultaneously means that members of the fire team can engage threats with other members of the team downrange because the muzzle of the weapon will not pass over the team

Trigger finger "indexed" on AR

member and the trigger finger will only activate the trigger when the gun's sights are aligned with the threat. In the dynamic chaos of a gunfight, profound in shock and noise, these skills can prevent an unintended discharge that might have tragic consequences.

TRIGGER FINGER MANAGEMENT

Trigger finger management means not putting the trigger finger inside the trigger guard until the gun is actually aimed at the target. The trigger finger should be "indexed" along the frame of the gun just above the trigger guard opening, pointed in the direction of the muzzle of the weapon. It is unfortunate that for many decades some trainers allowed shooters in basic training to keep their trigger fingers inside the trigger guard, trusting the mechanical safety if the gun was equipped with one (or luck if not) to prevent negligent discharges of the weapon. This is made worse by television and movie producers who persist in showing close-up shots of actors with trigger fingers curled tightly around the trigger even with no target in sight.

PRECISION MUZZLE MANAGEMENT

The second most important safety technique for group shooting in a 360-degree threat zone is constant attention to where the muzzle of the weapon is pointed. The most important principle of muzzle management is to never let the muzzle of your weapon pass across a fellow team member. Firearms instructors have different ways of communicating this principle. Sometimes it's called a "sweep" (as in the muzzle is "sweeping" across the body of the team member). Sometimes, instructors have students imagine that the muzzle is a laser beam and teach them to avoid the imaginary dot crossing the body of a team member. This would be the dot "painting" the fellow team member.

The most important principle of muzzle management is to never let the muzzle of your weapon pass across a fellow team member.

A useful training tool in reinforcing the importance of not crossing the body of a fellow team member with a weapon is to encourage each member of the team to remind the others with the simple expression "muzzle safe" or simply—"muzzle." Small violations of the muzzle safe rule are common at the beginning of team training and best addressed by the other members of the team.

MECHANICAL SAFETY ENGAGEMENT

The third critical safety technique for group shooting in a 360-degree threat zone relates to tactical engagement of the mechanical safety. All carbines and long guns have a mechanical safety. Most combat-capable semi-automatic pistols have a mechanical safety. The safety should always be engaged (set in the "on safe" position) unless the gun is actually aimed at a specific target.

Using the mechanical safety in addition to indexing the trigger finger along the frame of the gun remains a matter of some controversy in professional shooting circles. Law enforcement generally demands that the mechanical safety be engaged (reset to "on") after each threat has been neutralized and a visual scan of the area for additional threats has been completed. Elite military operators are often trained to leave the mechanical safety "off" when in contact with multiple threats until they are sure that the area is clear. In my opinion, unless you are trained to the razor's edge precision of a Ranger, Green Beret, SEAL, or a Marine Force Recon operator, use the mechanical safety *and* the indexed trigger finger to maintain a redundancy of safety practices.

The safety should always be engaged (set in the "on safe" position) unless the gun is actually aimed at a specific target.

PRACTICING ADVANCED FIREARMS TECHNIQUES

The best way for a fire team to learn these skills is under qualified professional instruction in the "shoot house" or on a "jungle lane" type course. The shoot house is a specially constructed range facility where teams can enter a room or area and engage multiple targets simultaneously using their combat arms and full power ammunition. The best commercial shoot schools have live-fire shoot houses but generally limit their use by multiple shooters at the same time to military and law enforcement members due to liability issues. A jungle lane is a trail in a wooded or brushy area with metal target plates hung at different distances and elevations from the trail. The fire team enters the shoot house or jungle lane and practices engaging targets at various angles and distances sometimes with other members of the team downrange. This type of training must simulate, to the most realistic extent possible, the fact that the shooter who is closest to the threat is not always the shooter who sees the threat first. Any member of the team must be able to instantly neutralize a threat whether or not he happens to be the closest fire team member to that threat.

The good news is that a recent development in firearms simulations—Airsoft guns—have now put live fire team training within the reach of every civilian fire team. Training with Airsoft guns is explained in detail in chapter six.

 TRAINING EXERCISE

1. Purchase "Airsoft" replicas for your team's combat carbines or rifles.
2. Create a "jungle lane" course using plastic plates (see chapter six).
3. Practice *individual* shooting skills emphasizing the safety techniques in this chapter.

Objective: To establish a strong basis of individual shooting safety skills

PART 2

EQUIPPING YOUR FIRE TEAM

5 *SELECTING UNIT STANDARD EQUIPMENT FOR YOUR FIRE TEAM*

Unit standard is the concept of standardizing firearms, uniforms, and support equipment for the three-shooter fire team. It seems painfully obvious that if one member of the fire team has a VHS portable radio and the other two have GMRS portables, communication will not be effective. It is deadly obvious that if all three shooters have primary weapons that use different caliber ammunition or even the same caliber with guns that take different magazines, the group will not be able to support each other with magazine sharing. If members of the fire team have personal medical kits that are haphazard in their contents, the ability to quickly deal with a multiple-wound crisis would be compromised. Unit standard represents the discipline necessary to plan for contingencies and make rational decisions prior to fire team deployment.

When social collapse occurs, it is too late to make reasoned decisions regarding common weapons, calibers, uniforms, communications, combat ruck contents, and medical kits because the ability to purchase equipment that matches the unit standard will have evaporated along with traditional law enforcement. Decisions regarding unit standard gear should be made in the pre-crisis training phase of fire team development.

This chapter outlines key equipment principles for a fire team to help your team identify the best unit standard for its skills and needs. Decisions on what equipment should be designated as unit standard should be based on:
- careful research
- open deliberation
- pre-crisis planning

UNIFORM FIRE TEAM ATTIRE

Warriors have known for centuries that to fight like a team you must look like a team. A common uniform serves two purposes:

- provides confidence to the members of the team
- dramatically increases the impression that the team is effective and well prepared.

Remember, appearance is a very important tactical element in achieving voluntary compliance. The ideal objective of fire team preparation is to present an image that is so competent and threatening that looters will move on to a softer target without physical altercations. When each member of the team appears in a common uniform and is familiar with the weapons and support equipment carried by their teammates, the chances of projecting a competent deterrent dramatically increases. Fire team members who have a common appearance simply look more prepared than if their appearance is not similar. Another tactical benefit of a common uniform is that if your position is being scouted from a distance, it will be difficult for curious eyes to determine how many men you have at arms.

Clothing for survival shooting as a team should be selected with both practical and political considerations. Basic battle wear should be comfortable and durable with many pockets. This does not necessarily mean "paramilitary." Think very carefully about choosing camouflage battle dress uniform (BDU) style garments for your team if you live in an anti-gun and anti-cop region. In a natural disaster or regional social collapse that affects an urban or suburban area, your fire team may still encounter organized law enforcement. Appearing in camo is likely to cause law enforcement to initially view you as a threat.

It is a serious tactical mistake to present a threatening appearance to police no matter how pro-law enforcement you may be at heart. And it's not just camo that can be dangerous. The all-black "Ninja look" may appear just as threatening to law enforcement. At the very least, in an anti-gun town, individuals who look threatening to law enforcement may be disarmed. Their weapons may be confiscated whether probable cause or legal basis for the confiscation exists or not.

 DEFINITION

Sniper Veil: A net fabric in muted colors worn over the head to disguise the shape of the shooter.

In a rural environment, law enforcement is far more likely to accept fire team members as good citizens because of a general acceptance of guns. In rural areas, local hunters wearing camo are a common sight during hunting season. In an urban or suburban environment, it's better to dress like Eddie Bauer than Rambo. A tactically acceptable, bland-appearing fire team uniform might consist of:

- light-weight, wicking underwear
- body armor, if available
- wool tactical pants, common color for all team members
- wool long-sleeved shirt, common color for all team members
- any good-quality, high-top boot in brown waterproof leather
- wool socks, two pair (one in ruck sack in plastic baggie)
- ripstop nylon, hooded windbreaker, common color for all team members
- down sweater or fleece jacket (in ruck in plastic bag)
- sniper veil (color to match likely terrain)
- black baseball cap with a sport's team logo or insignia
- leather or wool "fingerless" gloves

The benefit of this type of uniform is that its threat impression can be easily modified based on the situation. When worn with a combat ruck, knee pads, chest rig, weapons, and sniper veil, the appearance becomes very intimidating! Removing all exterior battle equipment but keeping a high-capacity, semi-auto pistol with four extra magazines concealed under the windbreaker renders the appearance quite benign. (It is impossible to make camo or all black appear benign no matter what equipment is visible.)

UNIT STANDARD FIREARMS

The choice of firearms in a fire team context is broad, and the decision about which weapons to make unit standard can have very significant unintended consequences if not made carefully. The most serious challenge to unit standard firearms is the problem of significant variations in gun-handling skills among team members. The decision on unit standard firearms also has financial implications. If the team decides on semi-custom handguns and top-of-the-line combat carbines with a .50 cal sniper rifle and an auto-feed combat shotgun as support weapons, the cost can easily exceed four thousand dollars per shooter.

The difference between "best" and "perfectly adequate" firearms can mean a much better balance between firearms cost and food, shelter, and water storage/purification costs. It does little good if the expense for firearms depletes the amount that can be spent on other necessities of survival. The defensive-only ethic of a fire team requires that its weapons are used to protect what it has stored, not steal from somebody else because the team spent too much on guns and not enough on grains.

Select a Common Caliber

At the very minimum, if you are going to take your role as a fire team seriously *all fire team unit members should have primary weapons of common caliber.* In the wake of a disaster or social collapse, there's a strong possibility that at least one fire team member will lose his ammunition reserves before the group assembles at the fortified residence. Knowing that the team has ample reserves of common caliber ammunition stored in different locations is very comforting. Also, the larger the purchase volume, the lower the cost of the ammunition. Its important to stock your ammo well in advance. The recent panic-buying of ammunition, leaving most retail shelves bare, is a good lesson for us all. Pick one caliber, combine your orders, and buy in bulk.

Select a Common Manufacturer and Model

The most desirable approach to unit standard firearms is to establish a common weapons platform (i.e., the same model gun from the same manufacturer). Guns do occasionally break. If a common platform for the primary weapon rifle/carbine and pistol is chosen, it is easy to store spare screws, springs, and firing pins along with clearly written repair instructions. Another advantage of unit standard guns of the same model from the same manufacturer is that the most mechanically inclined team member can become a capable unit armorer. If the team has a hodgepodge of weapons, the chances of bringing a broken gun back into service after a simple parts failure is virtually impossible because of the variety of spare parts and specialized tools that would need to be stored.

And a more mundane but still important consideration, when guns are common platform, cleaning after shooting becomes much easier because any problems with takedown or reassembly can be covered by a team member who is simply more adept at this tiresome but essential task. When all team members clean their guns at the same time, the guns actually get cleaned. With the "I'll clean it when I get home" attitude, sometimes guns get cleaned and sometimes they don't (as every police firearms instructor can readily attest). As department firearms instructors know, most of the "busted" guns they receive from cops are caused by dirt.

AR Semi-Automatic Rifles

Although it is a very serious mistake to equip fire team members with weapons based on some arbitrary concept of what is the most effective (i.e., "popular")

Top: 12-gauge pump-action shotgun. Middle: .223 caliber AR-15. Bottom: Bolt-action rifle.

assault-type firearm as demonstrated in movies or magazines, it is hard to find fault with the AR semi-automatic rifle as the most effective and adaptable platform. The dominant AR caliber .223 is mild in both recoil and report, that is the sound of the gunshot. For our purposes, .223 (the commercial designation) and 5.56 (the military designation) describe the same cartridge. Although .308 is becoming more popular on the AR platform, the shooter is the most important element of the weapons system and "too much gun" is actually worse than no gun at all because faulty tactical decisions may be made based on what the weapon can do in expert hands, not what the average shooter can do with it.

If the back door to your fortified residence is guarded by a shooter not entirely confident in his weapon, and the guard chokes under assault, the whole group is compromised. The AR platform in .223 is so mild that most shooters can accommodate to it well. Rifles or carbines in .308 are tougher to manage without a heritage of high-power rifle use in the hunting fields or on the target line.

In a worst-case scenario, novice shooters can be very dangerous to themselves or their fellow team members if they are afraid of or unsure of the weapon assigned to them. They can also be a danger if the weapon's manipulation is complex. In my experience as a firearms instructor, I've found that it takes about ten hours in the classroom and on the range to train cops to use the

AR-style patrol rifle with a basic degree of safety and effectiveness. It is an easy gun to train with. An additional benefit of the AR is that it can be matched with an Airsoft "clone" for tactical training purposes. (More on this later.)

If you will be defending an area that is more open, or live in a state that does not permit ARs, equipping each fire team member with both a sturdy bolt-action rifle in a common caliber *and* a cut down 12-gauge pump-action shotgun is not a bad alternative. Interestingly, with the current prices of ARs, this two-gun option may actually be cheaper to acquire.

Gun Safety in the Fortified Residence

Good friends forced by necessity to use firearms to defend themselves or dependents under their protection come in all shapes and sizes, varieties of shooting experience, and differences in the willingness to use aimed fire on human assailants. Every person in the group above age nine needs to be familiar with the basic principles of firearm safety because guns will be constantly within reach in a fortified retreat scenario. This means that every gun is always considered loaded, and never handled in such a way as to accidentally endanger another member of the retreat. A variation in the range of shooting skills is best addressed by basic firearms proficiency training. If all adult members of the survival retreat have basic firearms skills, and the members of the fire team have advanced tactical skills, the stage is well set for subsequent team shooting training.

So think carefully about how you will arm the fire team, but don't get caught up in the mystique of any particular weapons system. I would choose three shooters with great tactical skills and simple bolt guns backing me up over three gun-shop commandos with ARs any time.

UNIT STANDARD RADIO COMMUNICATIONS

Chapter eleven provides instruction on the tactical use of radio communications. Effective radio communications can dramatically improve the tactical efficiency of the civilian fire team, *if the team learns to use them in a disciplined way*. When it comes to selecting unit standard radio gear, the array of hardware options has grown dramatically in the last decade. The essential compromise remains portability verses range. Following is a description of four tactical radio options (Note: All range estimates approximate.):

Family Radio Service (FRS)/General Mobile Radio Service (GMRS) Radios: These devices are ultra-portable and offer two-way communications similar to a walkie-talkie. They have a range of 100 yards (91m) in heavy cover, 10 miles (16km) line of sight. No license is required to use them. FRS/GMRS portables are perfectly adequate for communications from one firing position to another on opposite sides of a fortified residence. They should be considered minimum essential "kit" for the serious fortified residence.

Citizens Band (CB) Service Radios: Like the FRS/GMRS, CB radios offer two-way communications similar to a walkie-talkie. They do require a belt carrier. Their range is a half mile (804m) in heavy cover, 50 miles (80km) line of sight.

Very High Frequency (VHF)/Ultra High Frequency (UHF) Radios: These radios also offer two-way communications and require a belt carrier. They have a range of 10 miles (16km) in heavy cover and regional with repeaters. The downside is that they require a complex and expensive licensing process for practice.

Shortwave Radios (Ham Radio): These are available in an ultra-portable model. The range is unlimited (with repeaters). However, they require extensive training and federal license to operate legally.

All four options require a carefully fitted earbud and boom microphone combination. All require frequent battery changes to retain good range. Again, this is where unit standard is important. If all the radios use the same battery type, you can store ample amounts of that battery at the fortified residence and have confidence that you can find the battery you need in a moment's notice.

Shortwave Portable Radio

In a prolonged power outage or social collapse, one of the first casualties will be broad situational awareness of the scope of the disruption. People who pay attention to the news in normal times will be frantic to gain information about the depth of the problem and the estimated time likely until rescue or reconstruction. Small portable AM/FM shortwave receivers are available at a modest cost, and with a steady supply of AA batteries, can provide access to international news. (Check with Radio Shack.) It could very well be that the BBC in London will be the source of the most realistic information on an American disaster.

 TRAINING EXERCISE

1. Collect all the firearms owned by your team and determine commonalities and/or group interest.
2. Identify a common rifle/carbine and handgun.
3. Review radio options and purchase three push-to-talk units and one portable AM/FM shortwave receiver.

Objective: Take specific planning steps for common weapons and comms

6 TRAINING WITH AIRSOFT GUNS

A recent development in firearms simulators has now put live-fire team training within the reach of every civilian fire team. These simulators are called "Airsoft" guns and they should be included in the training regimen of every fire team. Airsoft guns (abbreviated here to "AS") are replica firearms that closely duplicate the size, weight, and mechanical functioning of combat arms but use battery-powered air compressors to fire ceramic BBs.

AS guns duplicate the feel and function of the most popular semi-automatic handguns and the ubiquitous AR platform of .223 caliber carbines and rifles. Using AS-ARs the fire team can practice tactical maneuvers and aimed fire against targets spread around a 360-degree threat zone with relative safety using guns that almost exactly duplicate their primary defensive platform. It's important to note that while shots from an AS gun likely won't break the skin, the pellets do sting when they hit, and eye protection should always be worn during training.

After your fire team has selected its unit standard weapons, invest in a metal AS clone for each weapon. A metal AS clone for your AR gun costs no more than a good set of sights, and should be considered a must-have accessory to the full power gun. AR Airsoft replicas are also available in plastic, but they do not adequately replicate the feel of the real gun.

At this point, I must emphasize that without live-fire tactical practice as a group, the fire team will never develop the unit cohesion and mutual trust necessary to survive small-unit action combat. Civilian fire teams are not born after the crisis hits, they are born when they begin a regular training regimen.

Because AS clones are so inexpensive and readily available, *no fire team should ever engage in tactical training using centerfire or rimfire firearms!* The risk of injury or death through unintended discharge remains constant. Thanks to Airsoft, it's a risk that does not need to be taken to maintain fire team training standards. The team can and should practice marksmanship with their full-power weapons, but never with fellow team members downrange to the targets.

Civilian fire teams are not born after the crisis hits, they are born when they begin a regular training regimen.

A DISCRETE WAY TO TRAIN

In addition to the safety factor, using AS-ARs for practice is also very discrete. Although Americans are blessed with a wonderful National Forest system and plenty of BLM land (government land where safe shooting is legal under the jurisdiction and policies of the Department of the Interior, Bureau of Land Management), three shooters who are rucked up and firing .223 semi-autos are likely to draw complaints from observers and can cause contact with Enforcement Rangers who may take a dim view of the proceedings. Some of us are even more blessed with access to large private ranches or landholdings where live fire .223 practice is safe if well supervised. It is also possible that professional shoot schools will become more aware that a strong market demand exists for this type of training and provide appropriate courses for civilians whose skills they know from past training courses. These opportunities may exist but are unlikely for most shooters interested in learning 360-degree threat management. AS-ARs provide a discrete and inexpensive alternative for group training that so closely replicates the mechanical use of the battle weapon that switching from the AS to the battle weapon during a social collapse circumstance will be as smooth as possible.

Fire team members can adequately prepare for firing behind themselves without distraction only if they regularly practice shooting from the center of a 360-degree threat zone.

Fire team members can adequately prepare for firing behind each other without distraction only if they regularly practice shooting from the center of a 360-degree threat zone. Effective fire team operations is based on common tactics and good communications but most importantly, trust. That trust is the product of many training exercise replications. With AS-ARs, any fire team, anywhere, can have low-cost, discrete practice opportunities limited only by their imagination and dedication.

TIPS FOR TRAINING WITH AIRSOFTS

I regularly train with my AS-AR in my garage and yard and have some observations that may enhance the training experience for others.

- Do *not* remove or repaint the orange muzzle break. This keeps the AS-AR's clearly separate from the real thing.
- The best targets for practice are plastic saucers and plates (trade name Melmac) available at big-box discount stores. The plates make a resounding "ping" when they are hit and are very durable. Simply drill a hole in them, run heavy fishing line through the hole, and use it to suspend the plate from garage or basement ceilings indoors or bushes and trees outdoors. (Check your local ordinances as to the legality of discharge of a BB gun or pellet gun in your yard.) Melmac plates suspended on heavy-duty fishing line swing provocatively when hit. This makes them more challenging to engage. The longer the string, the more the swing.
- Use biodegradable pellets when available. They disappear in the yard and are easy to sweep up in the garage or basement.
- Do *not* play around with the AS replicas. Many can fire "full auto," which is amusing but has no place in fire team training. *Be serious in your training if you are serious about the outcome.*
- Be creative in your training scenarios. Paint the target plates camo colors or flat black to make them hard to find and hard to hit.
- Paint some plates red to represent a don't-shoot target and hang it in front of the real target to represent a hostage scenario.
- Gradually increase the degree of difficulty in placing the targets to add progressive challenges to the course.

AIRSOFT TRAINING EXERCISE: THE STACK

The use of Airsoft can be just as stimulating as battle combat weapons if it is taken seriously as amply demonstrated by the following scenarios I use with my students. One of the best group exercises using AS-ARs is one I call "The Stack." (A *stack* is a term sometimes used by special operators to describe a tight-line formation used to set up for an entry into an area assumed to contain armed threats.) This exercise takes place indoors, at night, involves the entire team, and requires an assistant.

Setting Up The Stack Exercise

1. The assistant first rigs at least nine plastic plates around the interior of the room at different distances and elevations and then exits the room and turns off the lights.

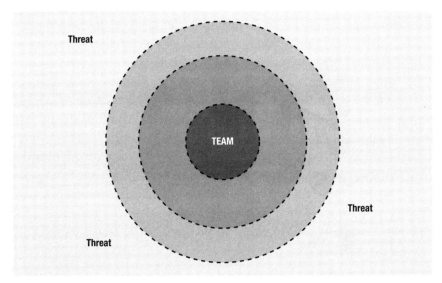

Zones of threat

2. The assistant then guides the fire team to the center of the dark room where they stage in a straight line, arm's-length apart.
3. After a pause, the assistant then turns on the lights, which acts as the "go" signal for the team to engage the targets.

Exercise Objectives

The learning objectives for The Stack are:
- Team members instantly divide the room into "threat zones" that do not overlap (see the diagram).
- Each shooter yells out the word *Tangos* (code for enemy targets) when he identifies a target in his threat zone.
- Each shooter fires *one shot* at each tango in his threat zone until all plates are hit.
- After all plates are hit (indicated by a "ping" and swing) each shooter gives the all-clear signal—"Clear front!" "Clear sides!" "Clear back!"
- After declaring "clear," the shooters remain in the "high-ready" position, scanning for other threats.

At no time in the drill should any shooter
- sweep
- fail to manipulate the safety properly
- fail to index the trigger finger between shots

The assistant will observe for safety violations.

Occasionally, the assistant should set up the targets so that one shooter has no targets in his zone. The assistant should observe this shooter to see if he continues to guard his zone or if he "poaches" targets that are in the zones of other shooters on the team.

In The Stack exercise, each shooter has his own threat zone that he or she should clear and then remains vigilant for additional threats. This exercise is an excellent way to train to employ all the advanced fire team safety imperatives (chapter four), gun-handling skills, and verbal communications (chapter eleven), and can provide a regular opportunity for members to train as a team.

AIRSOFT TRAINING EXERCISE: AS JUNGLE LANE

Another excellent training exercise is called the AS Jungle Lane.

Setting Up the AS Jungle Lane Exercise

In a wooded area or creek bed, hang ceramic plate targets so they are disguised or shielded in such a way that the shooter on *Point* (see chapter nine) does not see all of them.

The best terrain for an AS Jungle Lane is one in which brush or terrain features make it easy to hang plates in well-disguised positions. AS guns do not shoot ceramic targets well through even the lightest brush, and this limitation will require the shooters to quickly find clear lanes of fire to engage the targets. The search for clear lanes provides many creative opportunities to test the ability of fire team members to deal with tactical movement and different shooting positions, such as kneeling or prone.

To add even more complexity and intensity, the instructor can add painted plastic plates designed to blend into the background. The team must identify and hit these "hidden" targets as they pass through the course. The instructor should set the plates and maintain a count of those identified and hit. If the course is not shot "clean" (all plates hit), the team should run the course again.

Exercise Objectives

The learning objectives of the AS Jungle Lane are:
- The ability of the fire team to advance in proper patrol formation (explained in chapter thirteen).
- The ability of the team members to focus on their respective threat zones (explained in chapter nine).
- The ability of the team to communicate effectively using hand signals (explained in chapter eleven).

- The ability of *Point* to flank *Trail* to overwatch position (explained in chapter thirteen).
- The ability of *Slack* and *Trail* to effectively pick up and engage targets missed by *Point*.

The real versatility of an AS Jungle Lane is that once the course is set up, it can be run forwards and backwards, under different light conditions, and rotating all shooters in the team through the positions of *Point*, *Slack* and *Trail* (see chapter nine for an explanation of these three positions). (On my personal Jungle Lane course, I often fail to pick up one or two of the ten carefully painted and hidden plates as light and foliage conditions change ... and I hung them!)

SUMMARY

Use Airsofts to practice the three critical safety techniques for group shooting (indexed trigger finger, don't "paint" teammates, and proper use of the mechanical safety; see chapter four). Also use the Airsofts to practice giving hand signals while demonstrating tactical movement, and use them to practice different shooting positions. Regular team training using Airsofts on the Jungle Lane courses will provide the fire team with tactical training that is a step above even what most cops get. A dedication to regular group training spells the difference between living ready to cope and "posing" as ready to cope—what my colleague Creek Stewart, author of *Build the Perfect Bug Out Bag*, refers to as "couch preppers." So, get off the couch! You and your friends are not a fire team just because you own ARs and read this book. You are not a fire team until you practice as a fire team.

 TRAINING EXERCISE

1. Invent a new scenario using your AS "clones."
2. Test the team in reaction to the scenario.
3. Discuss how the team performed.
4. Repeat this process of inventing and executing new scenarios regularly.

Objective: Constant performance improvement

THE FIRE TEAM COMBAT LOAD

It is impossible to predict when a fortified residence or other defensive position might need to be quickly evacuated, and fire team members who are carrying only guns and ammunition could be forced to displace without support gear. Therefore, at all times, all fire team members should carry enough equipment on their persons to sustain combat operations over an extended period. At the very minimum, the unit's standard operating procedures (SOPs) should require that fire team members be fully equipped with combat ruck every time they set foot outside the defensive perimeter. Being "rucked up when gunned up," demonstrates a high degree of professionalism, presents a more imposing image to potential adversaries, and keeps the fire team better prepared for contingencies. Ruck up when gunned up. Get used to it.

Although a commonsense attitude should be used to maintain a balance between optimum mobility and equipment sufficiency, and some variations in combat load are expected based on personal preference and/or skill specialization, common combat loads should be unit standard. When all members of the fire team train with a full combat load, and regularly practice using the gear they carry, they will form a habit that could mean the difference between survival and failure in a sustained operational environment.

The combat load should be divided into four sub-systems based on how gear is carried. Each of the sub-systems should be carefully integrated so that the weight-bearing and attachment mechanisms do not conflict with each other while providing easy access to the most important equipment. The four sub-systems are:

- **Pockets:** escape and evasion (E&E) kits
- **Web gear:** ammunition, pistol, and personal medical kit

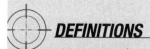

DEFINITIONS

Combat Ruck: A rucksack (European word for backpack) designed to carry enough support for at least twenty-four hours of combat operations.

Web Gear: A combat harness that carries spare magazines, canteen, pistol holster, and personal medical kit.

- **Combat rucksack:** equipment for twenty-four hours of operations
- **Relocation bag:** supplemental food and shelter supplies

POCKETS: ESCAPE AND EVASION KITS

Each member of the fire team should carry escape and evasion kits in their pockets at all times. Circumstances might require fire team members to "drop rucks" (ditch their rucksacks) or a team member could be without his backpack or web gear while in a sleeping position or during other inopportune moments. Under these circumstances, the escape and evasion kit is designed to allow the team member to escape a sudden assault and survive until reunited with other team members or escape back to the patrol base or hidden cache for replenishment of gear. Typical pocket contents for escape and evasion might include:

- BIC mini-lighter (fire starting, strobe signals)
- micro flashlight, CR2032 battery, red LED light (available from Radio Shack), and plastic tape (illumination)
- small container of insect repellent
- condom (used inside a sock to make an emergency water carrier)
- ½" (13mm) adhesive bandage tape, white, small roll (first aid, repairs)
- 12' (4m) paracord
- 1 small box raisins
- 2 packs salted peanuts (airline-style packaging)
- bandana, camo or dark color (used for bandage, face cover, gathering morning dew from grass, etc.)
- thin plastic sheet folded to 4" × 6" (10cm × 15cm) or "space blanket"

A knife is not included in the pocket list because a neck knife on a breakaway cord under the shirt is a more versatile means of carry and provides better access to it as a weapon of last resort.

WEB GEAR: AMMUNITION, PISTOL, PERSONAL MEDICAL KIT

"Web gear" is a generic term used to describe a harness-style, load-bearing apparatus on (or in) which magazine pouches, a pistol holster, personal medical kit, and other equipment can be suspended. Web gear can be in the form of a vest or shoulder harness, or in thigh pouches that are suspended from the belt with separate leg straps that secure the load to the thighs.

Excellent thigh pouches are available to carry primary weapon magazines, pistols, and medical kits. The advantage of thigh carry for these essentials is that thigh-carry pouches do not conflict in any way with the backpack or rucksack. Using thigh rigs for magazines, pistols, and medical kits also allows the use of standard, police-type, ballistic vests (when available) over which the combat ruck or backpack can be easily worn. See chapter sixteen for details on what to include in your Personal Medical Kit.

COMBAT RUCKSACK

A properly supplied and well-fitting backpack or rucksack can provide extended life support to fire team members without compromising their mobility. The ruck should have enough equipment to make a forced overnight away from the fortified residence tolerable. Note that I choose my words carefully here. *Tolerable* is not *comfortable*. The point of the gear in the combat ruck is to allow the team member to remain combat effective through the ordeal of several forced overnights away from base. If you carry enough stuff in the combat ruck to be comfortable in an overnight position, you probably sacrificed so much mobility that you would lose the firefight and never survive to enjoy the extra gear.

If the fortified residence is overrun, chaos will prevail and displacement (retreating) must be immediate. Under the pressure of making sure all dependent persons are safe, fire team members will not be in a position to make complex decisions about what to grab. Therefore, fire team members must have on their persons enough gear to shepherd their families safely to a fallback location or cache site.

I am often asked about the difference between a combat ruck and a Bug Out Bag (BOB). The simple answer is that all combat rucks should be BOB capable, but not all BOBs are combat rucks. In his book, *Build the Perfect Bug Out Bag*, Creek Stewart describes a BOB as "… a self-contained kit designed to get you through at least seventy-two hours of independent survival while on the journey to your destination." (I highly recommend this excellent book to help you understand the options for both BOBs and combat rucks.)

A combat ruck is designed to sustain combat operations for seventy-two hours, and the difference is significant. A BOB *may* include and support a handgun, but the combat ruck *must* support the main battle weapon. That means that the BOB has more room for benign equipment while the combat ruck should contain enough ammunition to sustain combat operations for the same seventy-two-hour period. Ammo is heavy. Ammo is bulky. (Makes the .223 look even more attractive, doesn't it?)

Another key difference between a BOB and a combat ruck involves tactical mobility. Stated as simply as possible, if you can't roll over five times with your BOB on, it just flunked the tactical mobility test. Every team member must be able to shoot from the prone position wearing the combat ruck and roll out of a threat zone to nearby cover if taking fire.

List C in this book's appendix includes a detailed inventory of the contents of my personal combat ruck. Use this simply as an illustration of what you could include in your fire team's combat ruck. Different needs, interests, and geographic areas may dictate other options. The most important thing about your combat ruck is that you *regularly hike with it and actually use the contents.* I hike and shoot with mine at least once a month on my Jungle Lane course, practicing setting up shelters and cooking meals in different locations and weather conditions. I cannot overemphasize the importance of regular practice; it improves your gear and your confidence with it.

Although some variant of the combat ruck should be part of the standard load-out for all fire team members, *all dependents over the age of six in the fortified residence should also have their own personalized backpack for emergency evacuation purposes.* The individual backpacks should be prepacked and labeled with the name of the dependent on different colored flags of duct tape. After filling the backpack with clothes, granola bars, toilet kits, books, water bottles, etc., add a small, lightweight stuffed animal as a comfort to the child. (Do not let the child see the inclusion of the little stuffed animal. This increases its psychological impact when used.) *Dependents' emergency backpacks are not for use for any purpose other than disaster evacuation.* Keep dependents' survival backpacks on a rack in your garage and on each child's birthday, open the pack, update the clothing, and rotate the granola bars and water bottles.

RELOCATION BAG

The purpose of the relocation bag is to provide for the possible forced relocation of the fire team and the dependents under the team's protection. A sturdy duffle bag with shoulder straps would likely be the largest man-portable container appropriate for this need. An army-style duffle bag is also an excellent choice if a tactical decision is made to evacuate to a government-regulated relocation center.

If you plan to use the bags for independent survival, select the contents of the bag by imagining what you would need if you were starting from scratch to create a secure structure or camp area. First priority in the relocation bag should be food; second is shelter enhancements. The relocation bag should not take the place of the food and other gear pre-positioned at the designated fortified residence or survival retreat. The relocation bag is for the contingencies of a forced relocation from the residence.

Food in a Relocation Bag

You'll be carrying this bag yourself while traveling on foot, so weight is a significant consideration for all the contents of a relocation bag. The most nutritional value relative to bulk is contained in processed grains and staples. Use resealable plastic food storage bags to double bag corn meal, rice, dried potato flakes, dried milk powder, refined sugar, and oatmeal. Popcorn offers high bulk for minimal storage. Be sure to include a multivitamin to supplement the nutritional value of the stored foods. Cooking these foods requires the proper utensils. Excellent, lightweight nested camping cook sets are available through major outdoors retailers.

Shelter in a Relocation Bag

If the secondary relocation involves several families, the most practical field-expedient shelters are family-size dome tents (lightweight and designed for backpacking) with a central cooking/eating/warming facility. Each family should have a relocation bag with a dome tent and one additional 12' × 12' (4m × 4m) durable plastic sheet. To erect a central shelter for cooking/eating/warming, your survival group will need at least one ¾ size axe, one ¾ size shovel, and one ¾ size bow saw. These tools are too big for the combat ruck, so keep them in the relocation bag. In a fire team that consists of three families (with three relocation bags), the larger tools and a heavy-duty pry bar can be divided between the three bags.

Preparing the Relocation Bag

Presuming that the fire team has already endured one relocation from their homes to a designated fortified residence, it may be impractical to have the relocation bags prefilled at all times. At the very least, the designated fortified residence should have the empty relocation bags ready with attached lists of what should be included on a secondary move if circumstances require one. If the National Guard does a security sweep through your neighborhood following or leading up to a disaster and gives you thirty minutes to evacuate, you need to have the bags and lists ready to go. However, make it a top priority to replenish each person's relocation bag as soon as everyone is safely settled in the fortified residence.

WHEELED HANDCARTS

It's a good idea for your survival groups to include a group-purchased wheeled cart that is stored at the fortified residence. These carts, sometimes called "gardener's carts," have two sturdy bicycle-type wheels on a central axle with a spacious box and a long pull bar. The carts are used to move heavy gardening supplies around the yard. Such a well-balanced wheeled cart could easily carry three relocation bags with a toddler or two sitting on top of the pile. It is entirely man-powered and completely silent in operation. (Remember, thousands of determined Mormon pioneer families made a 1,400 mile trek from Missouri to Utah with nothing but faith and wheeled carts.)

 ## TRAINING EXERCISE

1. Dress the team in combat uniforms with rucks.
2. In a safe location, *Point* (the leader) gives the command "Drop rucks."
3. Test which team members can find shelter and start a lasting fire with pocket contents (E&E kits) only.

(Do not disclose this exercise task in advance of the training.)

Objective: Test attention to detail and ability to overcome adversity

SELECTING AND HARDENING A FORTIFIED RESIDENCE

8

After you have your survival group and fire team assembled, you'll need to decide which group member's home most lends itself to defense. That home will be the team's fortified residence. Selecting the fortified residence likely will be the most difficult decision for a survival group. The homes the other families abandon for the fortified residence will be at greater risk for damage from looters, making it difficult for anyone to willingly leave their home when a fire team could potentially defend it. However, for the safety of the fire team and everyone in the team's survival group, the group should select the home that is easiest to defend and faces the fewest possible threats.

Some structures are more easily defended than others. Suburban, single-family, tract-style houses are especially difficult to secure because looters can easily approach through adjoining yards and use a fire bomb to burn you out. The most significant factor in selection of the fortified residence is likely to be defensible space. Space equals time—the more open space around your structure, the more time you will have to observe and engage a threat, and the greater distance at which that threat can be engaged, if necessary, with precision fire. The tactical concept of the "action curve" (where threat-engagement takes place) may be helpful to review to make the point. The action curve concept includes the principles that:

1. Open space around the fortified residence equals time to observe and react.
2. Reaction time puts you in front of the action curve, not behind it.
3. Being in front of the action curve means you are not reacting out of sudden surprise, but calm deliberation.

Other factors that might affect the choice of which house is to become the fortified residence could include:

- Two-story homes could offer higher shooting positions.
- Proximity to a natural water source would make water replenishment easier.
- A brick or stone structure might be more resistant to bullets.
- Fewer external doors mean fewer to block or protect.
- A fire-resistant roof might be beneficial.
- Ample room would provide needed privacy to multiple families.

(You may find it helpful for the team to review chapter fourteen on assault tactics to assess the vulnerability of your retreat.)

Use the principles in this and other books on the topic, and decide well in advance which of the houses is to be fortified. If that basic strategic decision cannot be made by the survival group, all other tactical decisions are insignificant. Identify the location of the fortified residence as soon as you form your fire team. It gives you a rendezvous point when a disaster strikes and allows your team to move equipment and supplies to the residence so it is ready well ahead of a crisis.

ESSENTIAL SECURITY MODIFICATIONS

Regardless of the fortified home's inherent strength or weakness, any modifications that increase security are worthy of consideration. *Barbed Wire, Barricades and Bunkers: The Free Citizen's Guide to Fortifying the Home Retreat* by F.J. Bohan is a helpful guide full of ways you can increase security at your fortified residence. Purchase and install basic defense items as soon as you identify the fortified residence.

Hardening of the typical residential structure generally consists of six elements:

1. window and door sheathing
2. external fire positions
3. impediments
4. signals
5. traps
6. decoys

Let's look at each element in more detail.

COVERING WINDOWS AND PROTECTING DOORS

You can easily create custom window coverings for each window in the residence. You will need:

¾-inch (2cm) exterior-grade plywood

table saw or hand saw

tape measure

drill

Torx or square head wood screws (several hundred)

special driver bits that fit Torx or square head screws

black flat-finish exterior house paint

4-inch (10cm) hole saw

1-inch (25mm) brass numbers

Step 1: Purchase ¾-inch (2cm) exterior-grade plywood and cut it to pieces that completely cover every window on the ground floor. Also cut pieces that will cover the bottom half of every window on upper floors. Be sure that each plywood window cover exceeds the actual window dimension by 4 inches (10cm) on each side, so that it can be mounted to the outside of the window frames.

Step 2: After the coverings are cut to shape, pre-drill holes along the edges so that they can be screwed to the outside window frames with wood screws. Purchase and store several hundred screws that do not use a standard Phillips head or flat head. (Use "Torx" or square heads.) This makes it more difficult for a potential invader to remove the plywood covers using standard tools. Keep plenty of the special driver bits for your battery drill/driver and at least four hand drivers that also fit the special screw heads. Although fastening the sheathing with a battery power drill/driver is the fastest method, be sure to have sufficient hammers and nails as a backup.

Step 3: Use a 4-inch (10cm) hole saw to drill round gun ports and observation holes through both sides of each window cover. Each covering should have two holes—one at 4 feet (1.2m) from the floor and another at 5 feet (1.5m) from the floor. From a standing position inside the house, a shooter should be able to look out through the upper hole and shoot suppressive or area fire through the lower hole. Position the holes next to the window frame so the shooter can position himself behind the wall to provide some additional protection from incoming rounds. The ports also provide a significant amount of natural light during the day and can easily be covered to prevent internal light from showing outside at night.

Step 4: Use a flat-finish exterior house paint in black to paint both sides and the edges of each cover to further protect the plywood from warping while in storage.

Step 5: Use a number to clearly mark each cover and its corresponding window. One-inch (25mm) brass numbers are available at hardware stores and are very durable when nailed in place. If you cannot reach second-story windows for exterior mounting, mount the plywood to the inside. This offers some protection for the upper floor rooms but does not protect the window glass.

Step 6: Store the plywood covers stacked flat in a dry area.

The easiest way to provide additional security to doors is with sandbags. It will take considerable preparation to employ sandbags around the exterior, but sandbags are so important a component in hardening a retreat structure that it is well worth the effort. At the minimum, two exterior doors (located on opposite sides of the structure) should be protected with a three-feet-high (1m) wall of sandbags on the outside of the (inward opening) door or across and outward of any alcove or exterior entryway. Sandbags provide a good visual deterrent and solid cover for a firing position if necessary. Three feet high is not too much to climb over for entry or exit of the structure.

Sandbag emplacement

The chief logistics challenge in being able to use sandbags for defense is storing sufficient sand. When disaster strikes, it will be too late to purchase sandbags and sand. The most practical way to store sand is to build a sandbox play area or a landscape decorative area:

1. Excavate a 12' × 12' (3.7m × 3.7m) square hole that is 12 inches (30cm) deep.
2. Dig holes and set posts in concrete every 4 feet (1.2m) around the structure for a 1-foot (30cm) wooden retaining wall around the edge of the hole.
3. Line the sides and bottom with heavy plastic sheeting.

This will create a sand storage area that will hold approximately fifteen cubic yards of sand (288 sq. ft. divided by 18 = 15). Fifteen cubic yards of sand will fill about two hundred sandbags. It takes fifty sandbags to make a small firing position. The sandbox can be used as a play area for the kids or an "oriental garden." (Unfortunately, every cat in the area will also want to use the box as a toilet. Sprinkle a box of mothballs on top of the sand and the cats will "go" elsewhere. But don't use this trick if you have young children who would potentially eat the mothballs while playing. In that case, consider building a cover for the sandbox or purchase a large plastic sandbox that comes with a cover.)

EXTERNAL FIRE POSITIONS

To effectively use the fire team tactics presented in this book, the fortified residence the team is defending must be protected by secure firing positions that allow the shooters at the corners of the structure to cover their zones from behind solid cover. An excavated, sandbag-protected "foxhole" from which defenders can cover all of the exterior walls of the structure is an example of this type of secure firing position. Don't plan on only shooting out of windows. Simply shooting from a window does not allow a defender to cover the sides of the structure without leaning out of the window to engage the attacker. (Not a wise or safe practice when you are under fire!)

Without protected exterior firing positions, you cannot effectively defend a structure. They can be hastily constructed, but materials must be stored pre-disaster.

Without protected exterior firing positions, you cannot effectively defend a structure. They can be hastily constructed, but materials must be stored pre-disaster.

Where you place your firing positions is crucial to the defense of the fortified residence. When placing your firing positions, it's helpful to take a page from history. Army forts built during frontier times had four stout walls and "blockhouses" at two opposite corners. These blockhouses extended above and beyond the walls allowing defenders to engage attackers that were taking cover next to the walls. Firing positions at opposite corners of the fortified residence need to be similarly situated.

Another critical factor in the placement of the firing positions is whether fire team members can get into the positions from the inside of the residence without exposing themselves to incoming fire. If possible, site your firing

Effective external firing position created with sandbags

position directly under a window or dig a trench from below the closest window to the firing position and protect the trench with a wall of sandbags. (Also hinge the plywood cover for that window so that it can be swung out to allow exit to the trench). With this setup, a fire team member can flop from the window directly into a trench and crawl to the larger and better-protected firing position.

To review, external firing positions need to meet the following qualifications:

- allow the defender to cover all sides and corners of the structure from behind solid cover
- placed so defenders can get into position easily and without being exposed to fire from attackers

Disguising External Fire Positions

It takes only a little bit of creativity and some stored materials to make your firing positions even more secure. The best enhancement is a covering or roof over the firing position made of plywood and more sandbags. (In a hot weather climate, you want the attackers, and not you, to be roasting under the direct sun.) Easily add firing ports to the walls of the firing position by leaving a small gap between a sandbag and then placing a plywood top over the gap to bear the weight of successive courses of sandbags or shoveled dirt that will be placed over the gap. When you contemplate firing positions, it becomes much easier to understand why so many sandbags and so much sand is required to construct them.

You can also use decorative planter boxes made from pressure-treated fir 2×12s as external fire positions. Build two parallel walls that are at least 3 feet (1m) high and spaced 1 foot (30cm) apart, and fill the void between the walls with dirt and rocks. Plant decorative creepers that cascade over the side of the wall that faces the street to disguise your firing positions.

Effective external firing position created with decorative landscaping

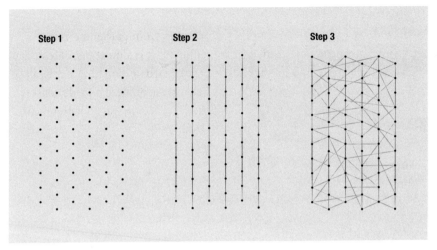

Tangle foot

IMPEDIMENTS

Impediments are nonlethal physical barriers that can block a mob from assaulting and ambushing your fortified residence. They slow down any potential attackers and reveal the attackers' locations so the fire team has more time to respond to the threat.

Barbed Wire

The most traditional impediment is barbed wire, which is available from any ranch or farm supply outlet. If you are securing a remote site, consider erecting a 6-foot (2m) chain-link fence around your structure at a distance of about 25 yards (22m) from the structure, and you can store rolls of barbed wire to install on the top of the fence when needed.

Tangle Foot

The cheapest and most effective field-expedient impediment to an assault by looters is called tangle foot. Tangle foot is a web of stiff black wire strung from 6 to 36 inches (15cm to 91cm) above the ground from vertical stakes. To install tangle foot, drive sections of steel rebar stubs well into the ground leaving 6 to 24 inches (15cm to 61cm) of the stub sticking out of the ground. Then string black rebar tie wire in random patterns from the tops of the stubs. (Stringing barbed wire from the tops of the 36-inch-high (91cm) posts discourages stepping over the lower wires.) Tangle foot is almost impossible to see at night, and *is* impossible to run through even in the daylight.

Bird Netting

Standard black, plastic "bird netting" (available from gardening retailers) is also a very inexpensive and effective impediment. It is almost invisible in daylight and completely invisible at night. Layers of bird netting hung across likely areas of assault will stop a runner cold. The purpose of these impediments is to stall looters in an exposed position so that they can be engaged with precision fire from cover.

Caltrops

Caltrops are an effective anti-vehicle impediment device if you have a long access road to your fortified residence. They are small, metal, three-legged devices that put a point up no matter how you toss them on the road and quickly deflate any tire that runs over them. Find a local welder or sheet metal fabrication shop and have some made up. The only safe way to store caltrops is in large plastic or metal containers. If properly made, they are very sharp. The purpose of caltrops is to stall a looter's vehicle far enough out from your retreat that you can engage them with long-range precision fire.

SIGNALS

Signals are electronic or mechanical devices that alert the fire team on lookout (a.k.a. designated sentry) to the possible presence of intruders. They can be divided into two basic subgroups: light signals and sound signals.

Light Signals

The best light signal is the M49A1 trip wire-activated flare device. This device is specifically designed to provide U.S. troops with a remote-activated, high-intensity flare illumination on the battlefield. When the trip wire is pulled, a spring-loaded firing pin strikes a shotgun-like shell that projects a very bright flare to an altitude of about 200 feet (61m). The flare gives off enough light to allow fire team members to visually identify targets at great distance so that defenders can engage the targets with precision fire. The device can also be rigged so that a defender can pull a trip wire to activate the flare at a distance from the defensive perimeter. (Warning: This device is a fire hazard.)

Several commercial sources offer inexpensive, battery-powered, motion sensor-activated lights. The best of the current offerings is the Mr. Beams wireless LED spotlight MB360. Sensor-activated, battery-powered lights on the four corners of your perimeter will provide plenty of notice to an alert sentry that the residence is being quietly probed in the dark. Be sure to store plenty of batteries for each device.

Sound Signals

You can create your own field-expedient, anti-intrusion sound-signaling devices from materials readily available at electronic stores, such as Radio Shack. This type of signal operates based on the electrical principle of the interrupted circuit. A magnetic switch normally keeps an electrical circuit closed, but attaching a trip wire to one part of the switch will cause the circuit to open when an intruder pulls the trip wire. When the circuit is opened, it activates a very loud screamer-type sonic alarm. The unit can be powered by a 12-volt lantern battery, which allows an excellent battery life because the drain when idle is very slight. One of the detriments of this type of device, however, is that once it is activated, it cannot be shut off without a defender leaving a firing position to physically de-activate it.

You can also make an extremely simple sonic alert device using a common spring-type rat trap and a trip wire. On a calm night, the snap sound made by the triggered trap is quite audible. Tin cans filled with pebbles and attached to trip wires are also quite effective as the Viet Cong ably demonstrated. If your survival retreat is in a rural area, be sure to have gravel sections in your approach road. Vehicles approaching over gravel make much more noise than on graded dirt or pavement.

TRAPS

Traps are mechanical devices designed to cause death or serious injury to enemies assaulting a defensive position. Traps should only be used in the complete absence of traditional law enforcement services, when a successful assault against your retreat has potentially lethal consequences, and when no other reasonable alternative exists to protect the retreat against attackers.

Traps must be used only in positions that are *never* used by fire team or survival group members (including young children). If you choose to place traps, keep a map of their positions in a prominent location inside the fortified residence so the exact locations of the traps are known by anyone who is or would become in charge of defense. One of the best ways to make a lethal trap less dangerous to your own troops is to put it in the middle of your tangle foot. No member of your survival group should have any reason to enter the tangle foot and certainly could not do so accidentally.

Warning: The deployment of potentially lethal traps even on your private property may subject you to criminal penalties. Know the laws in your area.

As an additional safety measure, a 2-foot (61cm) flag of blaze orange "surveyor's tape" or blaze orange duct tape should be placed on a 6-foot (2m) tall post within 50 feet (15m) of each trap. These safety flags will remind your fire team members and dependents that a trap is in the vicinity but will not disclose its exact position to the enemy. *Be very careful about where you set traps so that an ally cannot inadvertently trigger a trap in the heat of battle.*

Field expedient traps can include:

- "tiger pits" dug in likely lanes of assault with sharpened rebar stubs in the bottom and thinly covered tops
- trip wire-activated, spring-loaded spear-style devices
- break-open-type shotguns loaded with buckshot, cocked, and attached to wooden frames with a trip wire attached to the trigger

Traps can be camouflaged in many ways including use of native plants, spray painted black, covered with dirt, or any combination of the three.

DECOYS

Decoys are inert simulations of potentially lethal traps placed to deter looters and attackers from assaulting your fortified residence. It is possible, for example, to make a highly credible imitation of a Claymore mine out of painted wood. Decoys should be placed so that they are visible to any person who may be keeping your retreat under observation in preparation for a subsequent assault. If properly displayed, decoys should make all but the most desperate attacker think twice about the cost of the attack. The great benefit of decoys is that you expose no friendly forces to accidental injury. Three road flares spray painted light brown and bundled together with black plastic tape, attached to a pole outside your perimeter with a cord running toward your retreat should make any looter ponder greener pastures on the other side of town.

THE COMPLETE DEFENSIVE SYSTEM

The most sophisticated use of signals, impediments, traps, and decoys involves carefully integrating them into a coordinated anti-intrusion system. One of the best ways to disguise a trip wire, for example, is to put a clumsy decoy device with a thicker trip wire 6 feet (2m) in front of your real trip wire. Intruders will see and cut or step over the obvious decoy wire and then trip the thinner wire attached to the real trap because they think they know your techniques.

Think of your system as concentric circles. Light signals and decoys on the outer circle, impediments and traps on the inner. Always allow at least three completely clear lanes of escape from the fortified residence, but site these directly outward from your covered fire positions. Using that design, any assault using the unprotected lanes would be directly in line with a skilled shooter.

THE FORTIFIED RESIDENCE IN A PANDEMIC OR LIMITED NUCLEAR EVENT

The good news is that modifying your selected fortified residence to deal with a pandemic (fast-moving infectious disease) or limited nuclear event is not difficult or expensive. It is basically a function of protecting your defensive position from dust or germs. The point of this section is to offer you an opportunity to purchase and store some simple supplies to prepare for these contingencies. As I am fond of saying, "It's better to have duct tape and not need it than need duct tape and not have it."

In a post-Cold-War scenario the most likely adverse nuclear events are either a meltdown of a nuclear power plant (e.g., Fukushima following the 2012 earthquake in Japan) or a small dirty bomb from a terrorist strike. Dirty bombs are designed to be small—suitcase sized. The blast will crush structures and ignite fires in a radius of less than ten miles from the epicenter of the blast. But bombs are called "dirty" because they contain nuclear-reactive matter which will create a radioactive fallout zone much wider than the blast zone. The first warning of a dirty bomb will be a very bright flash (often compared to a second sun). If you are at home and see this flash, immediately yell; "Everybody down!" Looking at the flash can damage the retina and you must anticipate the possibility of an overpressure wave that could break windows and drop heavy furniture. Treat this exactly as you would an earthquake. Get your family down and under cover if possible. Meltdowns at nuclear power facilities are extremely unlikely to generate blast effects.

Nuclear fallout is simply radioactive particles released from a broken nuclear power plant or a "dirty" bomb. Nuclear fallout dissipates very rapidly but a massive early exposure or many small subsequent exposures over time can be quickly debilitating and eventually fatal. Think of nuclear fallout as "deadly dust," (dust that has an invisible glow of poison radiating from it.) All preparation enhancements for the already fortified residence are simply designed to increase your insulation from the deadly dust until their natural degradation removes them from being a danger.

The physical preparations for preventing radioactive particles and pandemic diseases from entering a fortified residence is similar and involves employing physical barriers. The simplest and most inexpensive barrier is made with clear sheet plastic and duct tape. After the initial blast, or warning of a nuclear event, immediately seal off all air conditioners, windows, and vents. If this means getting on the roof, make sure you have a ladder that gives you safe access. Have an assistant use a box cutter to cut the plastic sheet into sizes convenient for you to securely duct tape them to the vents or structures. Use duct tape liberally on exterior surfaces and use a heavy-duty staple gun on interior surfaces. If you're installing plastic sheeting against Sheetrock, you may need to add a thin wood strip to the Sheetrock to securely hold the staples to the wall surface.

Immediately following the alert to a pandemic or nuclear fallout, install plastic sheet in the following sequence:

1. roof vents
2. air conditioners
3. the inside surfaces of all windows
4. all external doors except one, which is your primary entry/exit door
5. internal doors and all vents into the "safe room," which is furthest re-moved from the external surfaces of the house (ideally, a bathroom or laundry room in the center of the house)

Your children may need to spend up to two weeks in the safe room, so prepare it accordingly. The primary entry/exit door (which should have sandbags that protect it as a firing position) should be protected with a buffer area sealed with plastic from floor to ceiling. The single opening to this buffer area should have at least 1 foot (30cm) of overlapping plastic on each side of the opening. Use this space to decontaminate all surfaces exposed to outside dust by brushing the dust from the surfaces. Leave the contaminated clothes and brushes in this area and dress in safe clothes once inside the second plastic sheet barrier. Make sure the suspended plastic sheets have at least a 1-foot (30cm) overlap on both sides of the opening.

Tracking Radiation

A ratemeter/dosimeter is an instrument that measures background radiation in your immediate area. They are available from many sources for around a hundred dollars. The Radiac Meter IM-179/U is one brand name example. (Be sure to store extra batteries if you invest in one.) Another options is a radiation-sensitive badge-style device that is worn around the neck. These are relatively simple and less expensive than a ratemeter, but not practical in this application because they measure cumulative dose instead of background radiation.

Because the most likely nuclear event will be limited in scope (e.g. a power plant release or a terrorist device), the most useful tool for tracking the spread of radiation will probably be a good quality battery-powered radio. Civil defense and FEMA technicians will make detailed surveys of background radiation and broadcast that information. A single-event release is far less difficult to manage than a strategic nuclear attack, and resources from outside the fallout region will be quickly mobilized and deployed. If you suspect that you are in the prevailing wind shadow of a likely target for a terrorist nuclear strike (e.g., container port, national treasure landmark, financial center) you may elect to invest in a ratemeter/dosimeter.

Evacuating After a Contamination

Should we run or should we stay? This important tactical decision needs to be made quickly following a nuclear or pandemic event. (You'll need secure communication lines between fire team members because cell phones will be jammed and landlines may be down.) Although it's impossible to accurately generalize how fast things will spread, you can estimate that fallout will travel at the rate of the winds aloft, which is not always the same as the wind speed at the surface. A safe estimate is the dirty dust will travel about thirty miles per hour from the point of origin. This should be adequate time for team members to apply the exterior sheathing of the hardened structure assuming that the necessary material is pre-positioned.

In the case of a pandemic, the most likely vector for deadly contagious infection will be through major international airports. Active government observation systems will likely identify the spread early enough for defensive measures *if you pay attention*. If you are convinced that a pandemic is happening, keep your children home from school and initiate strict shelter-in-place protocols. If your survival retreat is in a rural area and you can leave the city or suburbs in an hour, your team may elect to do so. Keep in mind that the people who already live in that rural area will also know of the pandemic and may very well elect to close access to their area. Every county sheriff has, in the back of their minds, a contingency plan for "buttoning up." The deputies and their many buddies with deer rifles and chainsaws (to fell trees to block roads) can do it too, so be careful about a "bug out" decision to avoid a pandemic unless you are well known to the sheriff and the locals. If you do get a foothold in a rural area, you will need both a fortified structure in the area and an "Alamo."

The best way to become known to the sheriff and the locals is to purchase property in their county and be a financial investor in their reelection campaigns. County sheriff's are elected (police chiefs are usually hired by city administrators), and because they are elected, they must pay attention to their major donors at campaign time. Attend an election event and write a big check. This *and* a copy of the deed to your property or other proof of residence might be your "pass" to get through the roadblocks.

Contamination and Combat Load

The primary responsibility for the adults in a survival group when faced with a nuclear or pandemic event should be to protect the children. The most likely debilitating effects of modest radiation exposure will not occur for years. Adults can afford that risk. Children cannot. Also, the effects of panic on a blissfully unprepared population cannot be overemphasized. The fire team will still need to post a guard and sleep schedule and may need to protect the fortified (and now insulated) residence from people who see your preparations and want to share them with you. Remember, you are likely to have the only house on the block with plastic covers on your vents and plywood on your windows—all of which serve as a big sign that says "safety inside."

Contingency planning to defend your stronghold through a nuclear or pandemic event includes necessary enhancements to your combat load. In a dirty-dust environment, the fire team will need to fight in gas masks and protective coveralls. This makes an already horrible task hellish and galling because your attackers will not have the same hindering attire. (The fact that they are dying of radiation sickness or Ebola is likely to only make them wilder because many of them will know that they have nothing to lose!)

Be sure that your mask has a provision that lets you drink out of your canteen. The best coveralls are army surplus chemical/biological/nuclear coveralls. They compress to a package about the size of a loaf of bread and can be carried with your web gear or combat ruck. When combined with the essential gas mask, they provide a good degree of protection against dirty dust. If this is not an option, use white painter's coveralls (pretty inexpensive and readily available at home improvement stores) for your coveralls. Buy many sets and dye them black and brown to camouflage them.

At the very least, your team should practice shooting in gas masks and ponchos or coveralls to have some experience in weapons manipulation under these specialized circumstances. I regularly practice running and shooting while wearing a mask, and it is almost impossible to describe how much the mask degrades your customary tactical proficiency.

 ## TRAINING EXERCISE

1. Pick the structure that will become the hardened survival retreat.
2. Inventory the supplies necessary to increase security.
3. Construct (samples):
   - one window cover
   - 6' × 8' (1.8m × 2.4m) of tangle foot
   - one battery-powered sensor light

Objective: Test methods of increasing security

PART 3

TRAINING YOUR FIRE TEAM

9 THREE TACTICAL ROLES

In a civilian defensive application, the ideal size of a fire team is between three and five skilled shooters. Three competent shooters represent the minimum number necessary to defend a fortified residence. Five is probably the maximum number of shooters who can be well coordinated by a designated leader. If you are facing a 360-degree threat zone, meaning threats can come at you from any direction, it takes at least three skilled shooters who are in constant communications with each other to cover all potential lanes of advance (which are approaches to the fortified home that could be used by would-be attackers). Four or five shooters is better, but three is the absolute minimum.

The examples and instructions in this chapter focus on a three-shooter fire team because that is the minimum necessary to prevent armed looters from surrounding the fortified residence and pressing an attack from more than one direction at the same time. However, you can apply these same principles to teams of four or five shooters as well. Given the effective use of communications, cover, and fire discipline, three competent shooters who are well practiced in mutual support can effectively resist many times their numbers of disorganized adversaries. Confidence in your abilities and the abilities of your team members will allow you to react to a lethal threat with highly focused aggression.

Group shooting as a tactical unit, what we are characterizing here as a "fire team," requires:

- the confidence to trust that your fellow team members can dominate their arc of responsibility with precision fire and
- the discipline to keep your concentration on your arc of responsibility no matter what is going on behind you

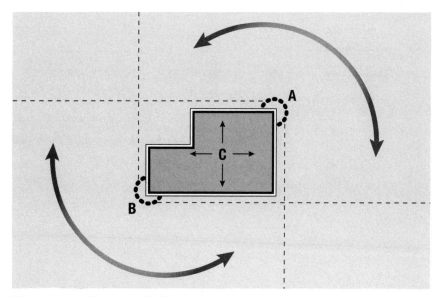

Three-shooter position in coordinated structure defense

This confidence and discipline can only be achieved with scenario-based, live-fire training on a range where targets can be engaged in a 360-degree circle.

THE THREE ROLES OF A FIRE TEAM

In a three-shooter fire team, each member will have a distinct functional role, which is best visualized in the context of a line of advance or patrol formation. The functional roles are:

1. **Point:** an effective leader and ideally the most proficient shooter in fast reactive fire
2. **Slack:** ideally the most proficient shooter in engaging multiple threats with rapid aimed fire
3. **Trail:** ideally the most proficient shooter in long-range threat suppression

Point is the shooter who is at the head of the line of advance and in overall command of the unit. *Slack* is the shooter next in the line of advance and second in command, and *Trail* is the shooter at the end of the line of advance.

Although the most common use of a fire team in a massive social-collapse scenario will be the static defense of a fortified home, the most effective way to train for using the three-shooter method is in a safe and discrete indoor or outdoor environment, where team members can engage with semi-disguised targets using non-lethal training guns to the front, sides, and rear of the three-shooter formation. Let's look at each function in a bit more depth.

DEFINITIONS

Line of Advance: The general direction of a patrol or tactical movement.

Patrol: A coordinated movement outside of the hardened defensive position.

Flank: The term flank means "side," as in the side of the formation or around the line of advance.

Covering Fire: Rapidly delivered high volume of fire into an enemy area designed to prevent them from aiming at the fire team.

Enfilade Fire: Stealthy movement to the flanks (exposed side) of an enemy position and engaging them with gunfire.

Hard Cover: A structure or material capable of stopping incoming rounds.

Incident Commander: A single person identified to be in tactical command of a squad.

Command Element: The fire team that includes an overall incident commander when more than one fire team is in contact with armed looters.

Assault Element: A dedicated group assigned to move and attack a defended structure.

POINT

The group member assuming the role of *Point* has the most important and stressful role in the three-shooter fire team unit. The *Point* is the accepted tactical leader of the team until he or she is rotated or incapacitated. This is because *Point* should be in the best position to visually observe risks and determine tactical responses.

Remember that according to our "SWAT" definition in chapter one, a fire team must have a clear tactical chain of command. A fire team is able to overcome and subdue an armed mob only through the use of coordinated defensive fire. Coordination under the hyper-extreme pressures of a gunfight is not achieved without that clear command structure, so it's vitally important that all members of the team recognize the leadership of *Point* and follow *Point's* commands.

Point Shooter's Duties

The role of *Point* in a patrol situation is to:

- Pick the route and navigate the line of advance using maps and terrain knowledge.
- Set the pace of advance relative to the threat exposure and difficulty of the terrain.
- Make tactical decisions about the disposition of other team members taking into consideration their skill levels, equipment, and the tactical situation.
- Use effectively aimed fire to eliminate any threats directly to the front of the line of advance.

All shooters should regularly practice the role of *Point*, but the most effective leader should be at *Point* in any situation in which contact with armed looters is possible.

The role of *Point* in a defensive application is to:

- Carefully assess the strengths and weaknesses of the defensive position.
- Confer with other members of the unit on the best tactical use of terrain.
- Assign shooters to positions of advantage based on their individual skill level and equipment.
- Confirm overlapping fields of fire consistent with traps, signals, and impediments.
- Identify a fallback position (also known as "Alamo") in case the primary defensive position is overrun.
- Set up the guard and sleep schedule.
- Monitor compliance with assignments.

Attributes of Point

The shooter at *Point* is the acknowledged leader of the fire team. Leadership in this capacity is defined as the ability to make both quick *and* good tactical decisions. Although the combination of quick and good tactical decisions in the face of lethal threat is the mark of an excellent combat leader, decisiveness, that is the ability to make a decision under extreme pressure, is the most important attribute of the *Point* member. Hesitation has killed more cops and special operators than bad decisions. A less-than-perfect decision made under the shock of fire can be modified as the fight progresses, but if *Point* is frozen with indecision in battle, movement from the kill zone is prevented, and the team's tactical response to the threat is frozen.

It is also important to remember that there are two kinds of decisions in a group survival situation—tactical and strategic. An example of a tactical

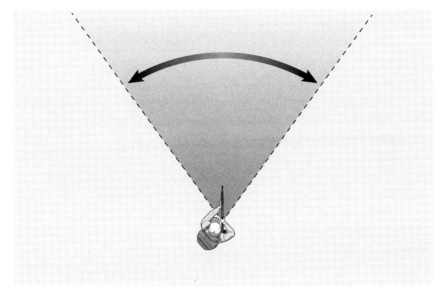

Zone of engagement for *Point* in patrol formation

decision is: "Peel left!" That's a command for team members to move to the left. An example of a strategic decision is, "This position may no longer be safe for our families. Should we relocate to a more rural area?" Tactical decisions are made on the fly by the leader and must be instantly obeyed. Strategic decisions should be made by the group in a process that involves open discussion and voting, with the leader serving as a moderator of the discussion.

In order to demonstrate leadership skills, the fire team member assuming the role of *Point* should possess the following attributes:

- calm reaction to suddenly changing conditions
- clear and concise communication skills
- mental and physical strength to maintain focus in a prolonged stressful environment
- respect for the opinions of fellow team members when group discussions of tactical and strategic decisions are possible

Zone of Engagement for Point

Ideally, *Point* should be the most proficient shooter in fast reactive fire (sometimes referred to as "CQB" techniques), but this skill is secondary to the mental qualifications of leadership. A less-proficient rifleman who is an outstanding leader can be armed with a shotgun while walking *Point*. The weapons system then compensates for a shooting-skills deficit. *Point* is responsible for

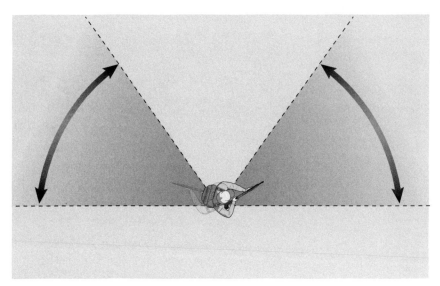

Zone of engagement for *Slack* in patrol formation

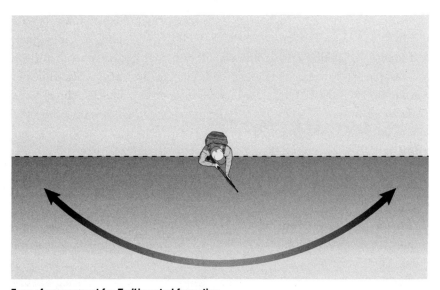

Zone of engagement for *Trail* in patrol formation

identifying and engaging targets in a zone approximately 20 degrees to either side of the line of advance.

SLACK

The role of *Slack* is to support *Point* and employ effective aimed fire against any threats in a zone from 20 to 180 degrees from the axis of advance.

A fire team in patrol formation

With only the most occasional exceptions, *Slack* should always remain within the line of sight of *Point* in order to receive and respond to hand signals and to observe if *Point* goes down. But *Slack* should not be so close to *Point* that one burst of fire from the looters could hit both *Point* and *Slack*. Ideally, *Slack* should be the most proficient shooter in engaging multiple threats with rapid aimed fire.

TRAIL

The role of *Trail* is to engage with aimed fire any threats from 180 to 360 degrees of the line of advance and be prepared to flank to the side of the line of advance to provide covering fire for *Point* and *Slack* as they advance and enfilade fire to eliminate threats. With only the most occasional exceptions, *Trail* should always remain within line of sight with *Slack* but not so close that one burst of fire could hit both *Trail* and *Slack*. Ideally, *Trail* should be the most proficient shooter in long-range threat suppression (sometimes referred to as "designated marksman" or "sniper" techniques).

FIRE TEAM CHAIN OF COMMAND

Point is always assumed to be in tactical command of the unit in both a patrol and defensive application. Because the combat environment is impossible to predict, and the shock of the armed encounter is profound, succession of command must be smooth and effective if *Point* is injured or suffers a catastrophic weapons failure.

Point Down

The essential tactical principle is that the team must never be without a leader. Succession of leadership should be an automatic and well-practiced behavior. If a fire team *Point* is no longer able to provide leadership, a situation known as "*Point* down," *Slack* should automatically assume command. The loss of *Point* represents not only a loss of one-third of the firepower of the team, but also dramatically reduces the capacity of the unit to deal with a 360-degree threat environment. Unless circumstances dictate otherwise, in a *Point*-down situation, all forward patrol progress should stop immediately and a defensive perimeter around *Point* should be established until the medical condition of *Point* can be determined. New *Point* (formerly *Slack*) should make a fast decision about whether to maintain a defensive perimeter to protect old *Point* for medical evacuation or immediately evacuate the scene to hard cover. When in doubt, immediate evacuation if possible is preferable to the sacrifice of the entire team.

Point Relinquished

Under certain circumstances, *Point* may voluntarily relinquish the position to *Slack* or *Trail*. This may occur when terrain features block the direction of advance of the patrol or if *Point* decides to exit the fortified residence to confer with neighbors or friendly forces.

In a patrol environment, rather than *Point* collapsing back on the unit, *Point* may signal *Trail* to flank to the right or left and assume the role of *Point* for the new axis of advance. This tactical change in tasking may last for as long as new *Point* (former *Trail*) is comfortable with the role. As soon as the tactical situation permits, a meeting can clarify the best options for continuation of the patrol.

If *Point* exits the fortified residence for any reason, designated *Slack* takes command of the actual defenses of the structure or defensive position until *Point* is back in position.

In an unknown-risk patrol environment, *Point* may occasionally rotate with *Slack* to manage the stress load. (Keeping one person as *Point* too long dramatically reduces the shooter's combat effectiveness through fatigue.) Walking *Point* is an extremely stressful activity when done properly and occasional rotation is good tactical practice.

COMMUNICATING IN A THREE-SHOOTER TEAM

In both patrol and defensive situations, it is imperative that all members of the fire team maintain effective communications at all times. Although tactical radio communications can be very effective, shooters should try to maintain visual contact with other members of the team and be well trained in the tactical use of hand signals to communicate complex actions in a stressful environment. Hand signals are important because they allow the fire team to operate silently and are a necessary default communications system in case tactical radio communications break down for any reason. Hand signals are covered in detail in chapter eleven.

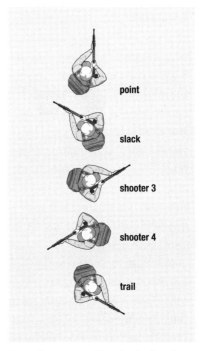

point

slack

shooter 3

shooter 4

trail

Zone of engagement for shooter 3 and shooter 4

ADDING A FOURTH OR FIFTH SHOOTER

A three-shooter unit is the minimum requirement for fire team tactics, but as I mentioned earlier, you can add up to two additional shooters to your unit. When two additional shooters are involved, they integrate into the patrol line of advance in position 3 and 4 with designated *Trail* remaining in the rear position. The tasks of shooter 3 and shooter 4 might include:

- engagement with accurate aimed fire of threats to the side of the line of advance (by prior agreement, each covers a different side of the line of advance)
- providing specialized support such as medical, trap and hazard neutralization, and/or protecting dependents who are being moved
- the carrying (transport) of supplies or materials

Auxiliary Shooters in Windows

When defending a fortified home, auxiliary shooters stationed in well-protected window positions can dramatically improve the fire team's capacity to provide overlapping fields of fire. Practice this formation with the auxiliary shooters using empty guns during the practice drill. Having them simulate aiming, firing, and reloading from their assigned position gives them confidence that they can effectively aim, fire and reload in a real-life situation. Identify the fortified home's cover positions that armed looters are likely to use during an assault and instruct shooter 3 and/or 4 to aim and fire at the cover position.

Remember that auxiliary shooters may have a strong psychological inhibition against precision shooting at specific human targets. "Precision shooting" is lining up the sights on a specific human target and pressing the trigger. Auxiliary shooters may be more effective in the delivery of "area" or "suppressive" fire. The auxiliary shooters are then defending an area with volume of fire, not eliminating specific adversaries.

Criteria for Adding Additional Shooters

Depending on the tactical situation, auxiliary shooters can be moved from one side of the house to another to provide defensive fire on the side under the strongest attack. Additional shooters may only be fully integrated into the fire team when they meet all skills requirements and have regularly trained with the original three members of the fire team. (Use the criteria found in chapter four to evaluate the person's ability to effectively join the team.) Do not attempt to incorporate new shooters into the team until you have actually seen them perform under stress with their weapons. Shooting effectively while moving is so rare a skill that, unless the fire team leader has actually observed the auxiliary shooter perform it, they should not be given this assignment.

WORKING IN A SQUAD

You may be fortunate enough that the survival group in your fortified home will include enough qualified shooters to form multiple three-shooter fire teams. Several three-shooter fire teams operating together is called a "squad." Fire teams within a squad are often designated by color, such as "Blue Team," "Gold Team," or "Red Team." Multiple fire teams acting in mutual support can be used in many ways:

A fire team is only as good as its Point.

- in rotation with other units on the defensive perimeter
- as in-line support of a lead unit in an axis of advance
- as a quick reaction force if another team comes in contact with looters
- as a flanking unit to provide security for a line of advance or effective enfilade fire

Creating Additional Fire Teams

The establishment of a second or third fire team in a large survival group is primarily determined by the quality of the available leadership for successive teams. A fire team is only as good as its *Point*. The general principle of dividing a large group of shooters into fire teams ensures each unit will have a designated leader, and the members of each unit will learn to have confidence in their leader. In the catastrophic sensory overload of armed encounters, the biggest killer is usually not enemy proficiency, it is the collapse of leadership. Dividing a large group of shooters into three-member fire teams formalizes the chain of command and helps maintain squad cohesion in battle.

Chain of Command in a Squad

In a squad composed of more than one three-shooter fire team, a single over-all "Incident Commander" should always be identified. Note: The incident commander may also be *Point* of one of the units, but if that is the case, his fire team should not assume the primary role in the engagement. If the squad commander is also a fire team leader, his or her fire team should be considered the squad "command element," and not the assault element or on the line in the defense of a hardened structure. The command element always stays to the rear of the action unless it must become a reactive force. If radio communications join more than one fire team while in contact, a designated radio operator should be assigned to the command element.

 ## TRAINING EXERCISE

1. Pick a park or recreational area with a variety of terrain and cover.
2. In rucks, but without weapons, hike cross-country (off established trails) in patrol formation.
3. Practice
   - hand signals (see chapter eleven)
   - flanking *Trail*
   - talk-it-over (see chapter eleven)
   - cover-to-cover navigation

Objective: Improve patrol skills

Advanced: Replicate exercise in the dark with red lights only

10 EIGHT AREAS OF TACTICAL PROFICIENCY

Regardless of which role the member plays on the fire team—*Point*, *Slack*, or *Trail*—every member of the fire team must be able to master, demonstrate, and clearly explain the following eight areas of tactical proficiency:

1. cover and concealment
2. fire and maneuver
3. flanking or enfilade fire
4. overlapping fields of fire
5. precision fire
6. covering or suppressive fire
7. combat communications
8. combat medic

This chapter will explain each area in detail and provide training exercises for improving team combat proficiency.

COVER AND CONCEALMENT

There is an important distinction between cover and concealment, and fire team members must understand the difference and clearly distinguish between the two in the heat of battle. According to *Street Survival: Tactics for Armed Encounters* by Ronald J. Adams, Thomas A. McTernan, and Charles Remsberg, concealment is something that obscures the fire team member from observation. Cover is something that will stop a bullet. An example of concealment would be a hedge of plant material. An example of cover would be a rock outcropping. Most cover is also concealing, but most concealment is not cover. In a gunfight, the use of solid cover is vastly more tactical than concealment, but in an absence of cover, concealment is better than nothing.

The use of cover has offensive and defensive implications. From a defensive position (inside a house, for example), team members must be aware of what structure actually offers cover. Two Sheetrock walls with roll insulation is not cover, it is only concealment. Even an external stucco or brick wall will not stop a .308 rifle round. Walls *and* sandbags or walls *and* ceramic fixtures or metal appliances may constitute cover. Most of a car body is concealment only and will not stop rifle rounds or full metal jacket (FMJ) handgun rounds. Engine blocks and steel wheels and transaxles will stop those projectiles and do constitute cover.

In a patrol environment, the tactical use of cover involves two skills:

1. the ability to identify cover positions ahead of you in the line of advance you are walking
2. the ability to move to cover in a quick bound under the protection of area or suppressive fire from other team members

FIRE AND MANEUVER

Tactical movement can be divided into three basic types:

- stealthy patrol
- bounds
- flanking and enfilade fire

Stealthy Patrol

Stealthy patrol is used when the team must move quietly for any reason. The essence of stealthy movement is noise suppression and slow, smooth movement. Stealthy patrol uses concealment whenever possible to screen the team from observation and cover to provide security. *Point* should manage stealthy movement using the following principles:

- scanning 180 degrees to the axis of advance to identify potential ambush sites, including binocular examination of cover to detect possible enemy hides
- picking a trail or track that is not the most obvious, (avoids traps and signals) and keeps the team close to cover in case incoming rounds are encountered
- flanking *Trail* member positioned to the left or right to protect the team in advances around corners or obstacles
- stopping frequently to listen for movement by potential attackers

Bounds

Bounds are used in a position at high risk for ambush. The first rule of bounding is *only one member of the team moves at a time*. The second rule of bound-

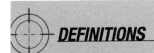

DEFINITIONS

Bound: A short rush from one cover position to another.
Precision Fire: Carefully aimed fire to engage a specific target.

ing is that movement is in *short rushes* of no more than five seconds duration. Bounds are limited to five seconds because that is the amount of time it takes for the average shooter to recognize, mount a weapon, and aim at a moving target.

Bounds should be designed to move the team from solid cover to solid cover (in a heavily wooded environment, for example). If bounds must be taken across an open or grassy area, each bound should end with a "drop and roll" to a position at least 10 feet (3.1m) from the drop point. Using that technique, when the next bound must be taken, it will begin from a position different from where an armed attacker saw the last bound end.

When bounding is used in the face of fire or to displace from fire, the other two team members should offer aimed covering fire to protect the bounder. Bounds should be initiated at seemingly random intervals, but never at so rapid a pace that the shooter who last bounded is not yet ready to offer covering fire for the next bounder.

The tactical use of enfilade fire is likely to be the most effective combat technique available to the civilian fire team.

FLANKING AND ENFILADE FIRE

As introduced in chapter nine, enfilade fire is a stealthy movement to the flanks (exposed side) of an enemy position and engaging them with gunfire. Flanking and enfilade fire are tactical maneuvers designed to take attackers by surprise. The tactical use of enfilade fire is likely to be the most effective combat technique available to the civilian fire team. Disorganized adversaries, mobs, and/or small groups of looters are likely to focus intently and exclusively on gunfire directly to their front and pay little or no attention to the possibility of incoming fire on their flanks. Sudden precision fire from the side is likely to cause significant casualties and break the confidence of the attackers, causing them to flee.

OVERLAPPING FIELDS OF FIRE

This is a military term for a concept that all lines of hostile advance must be covered by defensive fire and all incoming fire will immediately be answered with return fire.

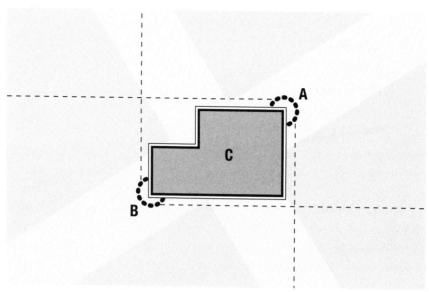

Overlapping fields of fire

PRECISION FIRE

Precision fire is the ability to eliminate the threat of an armed adversary:
- with a center-body hit
- in three seconds or less
- at distances up to 300 yards (depending on the firearm)

The effectiveness of precision fire is less determined by the caliber of projectile or action of weapon than by the ability of the shooter to maintain sight picture, trigger control, and a willingness to kill in a high-stress environment. Precision fire represents the ultimate combination of a shooter's skill and will. It is most dependent on the type of sighting system affixed to the gun. For this reason, although ideally the three shooters should have a common weapons platform (common manufacturer and model weapon), at least one of the platforms should be equipped with a telescopic sight of not less than four-power magnification. The rifle with this scope should be carried by *Trail*, although all members of the fire team should be sufficiently practiced in its use so they are able to engage threats effectively at significant distance.

It is a well-recognized battlefield phenomenon that, regardless of cause or need, many shooters will not actually aim at an individual enemy soldier. For some psychological reason, they will draw a breath or close their eyes or otherwise fail to engage a specific human target with aimed fire (*On Killing* by Lt. Col. Dave Grossman). Covering or suppressive fire saturates an area to keep the attackers' heads down so that they cannot return accurate fire. The fire team leader must understand that he may have only one precision shooter to depend upon—himself. That does not mean that other members of the fire team cannot make a vital contribution to the defense of a hardened residence if one is forced by circumstances on the team.

COVERING OR SUPPRESSIVE FIRE

Covering or suppressive fire is a well-established principle of military small unit tactics. This type of fire can allow precision shooters to move with relative safety to positions of security or advantage from which they can eliminate specific threats with carefully aimed shots. Covering fire is sprayed, not aimed. The spray of covering fire can be delivered into a relatively narrow kill zone, but any actual threat elimination that is the result of covering fire is more of an accident than a direct result.

COMBAT COMMUNICATIONS

Effective communication is the key to fire team survival when confronting larger groups with hostile intent. Two modes of communication—hand signals and radio "comms"—should be well practiced and integrated. This concept is so important that chapter eleven is solely dedicated to it.

COMBAT MEDIC

Every member of the fire team should have confidence that he or she can give and will receive effective emergency care in a battlefield situation. One member of the team should receive advanced medical training and become "team medic." Many police officers and military personnel have died from survivable battle wounds because they lost emotional control and panicked. Basic competence in battlefield medical care is so important that chapter sixteen is dedicated to it.

TRAINING EXERCISE

Perform this exercise on a Jungle Lane or inside a structure using Airsoft "clones." Using hand signals only, practice:
1. flanking Trail for enfilade fire
2. rotate *Point, Slack* and *Trail* positions

Objective: Test effectiveness of enfilade fire

11 TACTICAL COMMUNICATION SKILLS

Effective communications under pressure is essential to a civilian fire team's effective use of defensive fire. In fact, effective team communications is a very significant multiplier of force because, when each member of the team knows what the others are seeing and doing, the coordinated use of three to five guns could suppress the disorganized opposition of fifty guns.

There are five important elements of effective tactical communications for civilian fire teams. Because they build on each other, they should be learned in the following sequence like steps on a ladder:

1. shared vocabulary
2. hand signals
3. radio communications
4. codes
5. whistles (low tech)

SHARED VOCABULARY

It doesn't matter if you can use hand signals and radio comms if the members of the fire team do not share a common tactical vocabulary.

Dozens of tactical vocabulary terms are found in the glossary of this book. Each fire team member should memorize the terms in that section carefully. Vocabulary words like *Point, Slack, Trail, covering fire, precision fire, alamo, squad, bounds, overwatch, Blue Team, rule of 50, displacement, stealthy patrol, axis of advance, area suppression fire, unit standard,* and *snap caps* need to be understood so well that team members naturally include them in conversations with clarity of meaning and economy of wording. The only way this can be accomplished is with frequent scenario-based team training in which actually using the vocabulary places the words in a practical context.

This tactical vocabulary becomes a code unto itself. Armed professionals use tactical language because in the dynamic chaos of an armed encounter, winners communicate the most precise meaning with the fewest possible words.

Compare saying, "Steve, we're stuck here. Can you go around to the right about 40 yards, find solid cover and fire them up so that we can advance?" to saying: "Trail, enfilade, 40 right!"

The first command took twenty-four words and five seconds. The second command expressed the exact same instructions in only four words and one second. The word *Trail* identifies the shooter. The word *enfilade* automatically implies a flanking maneuver (engaging the enemy with fire from the side). The distance of the flanking maneuver and the direction of the maneuver are designated as indicated—40 (yards is implied) right.

The first command is easily understood by anyone listening in, and exposes a weakness the fire team is facing. The second command sounds very intimidating to anyone listening in and exposes no weakness. Remember, the main goal of a civilian fire team is to present a credible show of force that convinces would-be attackers to move on without any shots being fired. The use of precision vocabulary plays a huge role in presenting that credible show of force.

HAND SIGNALS

Hand signals are necessary in a patrol environment or in a house-clearing scenario to maintain noise discipline. The ability to communicate clearly and silently using hand signals is the mark of a well-trained fire team. Hand signals are most often used in communication from *Point* to *Slack,* and *Slack* forwards any signals from *Point* to *Trail* so the team can remain as quiet as possible in a patrol environment. Remember, *Point* is in tactical command of the team because he is in the best position to see the terrain ahead, navigate around obstacles, clear areas, and visually identify threats. When the team is in motion, *Point* should always communicate using hand signals even when the probability of enemy contact is slight.

Using hand signals correctly is a perishable skill. Regular practice keeps the use of hand signals fresh. There are sixteen basic hand signals that should be mastered by each member of the team, included here with their meanings:

Delivering Hand Signals

How hand signals are delivered can be just as important as what signals are given. *Point* should be expected to originate most hand signals because *Point*

16 HAND SIGNALS AND THEIR MEANINGS

Motion	Meaning
Fist	Stop
Five fingers spread	Disperse and take cover
Number of fingers held in the air	2 fingers designates *Slack*, 3 fingers designates *Trail*—can also indicate distance in yards of flanking movement
Pointing with index finger	Indicates direction
Hand flat against chest "wagged" up and down rapidly	I don't understand, or no, or cease fire
Thumbs-up	Yes, or I understand, or good
Fingers pointed at eyes	I see or look
Finger pointed at ear	I hear something
Finger pointed at sender	Me
Finger pointed at recipient	You

is in the best position to observe terrain and enemy activity to the front of the team. *Point* should deliver hand signals without taking his eye off the threat. It is the responsibility of *Slack* to be aware of any hand signals by *Point* in *Slack's* constant situational awareness. In other words, unless *Slack* is actually engaging a threat, he is responsible for picking up any hand signals originated by *Point*. *Trail*, unless actually engaging a threat, is responsible for picking up any hand signals originated by *Slack*. Hand signals usually progress rearward from *Point* to *Slack* to *Trail*. *Point* should originate the hand signal in the most discrete motion possible. *Trail* watchers can see sudden movement from a great distance.

Hand signals are best originated next to the thigh. Only use a high-arm position when members of the team are at their maximum visual range from each other.

Motion	Meaning
Finger pointed at ground next to sender	Come to me
Arcing motion of hand with fingers closed	Flank out
Tap of fist against thigh	Indicates distance in five meters per tap
Middle finger extended	CAUTION… I am held at gunpoint! Flank out and cover me
Index fingers from both hands making a "T" or index finger making the American Sign Language sign for letter "T"	"Tango" (code for enemy)
Index finger up and circled above the shoulder	Gather around me for a "talk-it-over"

Acknowledging Hand Signals

Hand signals can be acknowledged in three ways:

1. by performing actions consistent with the signal
2. with a nod of the head or thumbs-up gesture (this means, "yes" or "affirmative")
3. with a vertical "wag" of the hand with closed fingers in front of the chest (this means "I don't understand" or "no")

Actions consistent with the signal are an implied acknowledgment of the signal. If *Point* shows three fingers (sign for *Trail*, or third shooter in line) and gestures with his index finger to the ground by his side and *Trail* immediately moves toward *Point*, *Point* can safely assume that *Trail* got the message.

To confirm that a message has been understood and complied with, *Point* should take a quick peek over his shoulder to see either the implied acknowledgement or a wag (meaning, "I don't understand") responding signal. Upon receipt of the wag, *Point* should resend the hand signal. Another wag or a shake of the head indicates that the team member cannot comply for some reason. (This generally requires a displacement to cover and a quick talk-it-over.) When *Point* takes his quick peek, a simple thumbs-up or nod confirms receipt of the message.

Sending Hand Signals From Rear to Front
Under certain circumstances, hand signals may need to travel from the rear to the front of the patrol formation. *Trail* may hear or see looter activity to the rear of the team and need to communicate this with *Slack* and *Point*. A low whistle is a subtle enough sound to get the attention of the next team member, and the whistle can be followed with a hand signal. In this example, *Trail* would whistle to get the attention of *Slack* and point a finger to his ear if he hears the sound of pursuit, or point to his eyes if he sees something that puts the team at risk.

Convening a "Talk-it-Over"
Sometimes it is impossible to use hand signals alone to sufficiently communicate about a tactical condition during a patrol movement. It is very important that *Point* gets the input of his team members on complex challenges or navigational issues. Team members who understand better, fight better. To have a quiet group discussion (called a "talk-it-over") consistent with good sound discipline, the team member who wants the discussion indicates so with his index finger up and circled above the shoulder. Any member of the team can call for a talk-it-over at any time. *Point* can wag off the request if he needs to hold it off until better cover is found. If *Point* wags off the request, he should signal how many minutes the delay will take with fingers representing minutes. That assures *Slack* or *Trail* that *Point* has received the request and will comply at the first safe opportunity.

The talk-it-over should take place behind or next to hard cover.

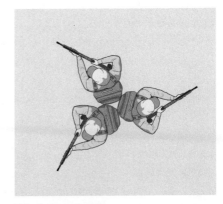

Talk-it-over position

All three fire team members should remain standing in a tight circle, facing outward, with their shoulders touching. This close proximity allows all conversations to be conducted in a whisper. Team members should not look at each other when they talk, their visual responsibility is the threat zone. All weapons should be pointed outward in the low ready position, and team members should be extremely vigilant for threats with each member responsible for one third of the 360-degree threat arc that surrounds them. (A tight group temporarily violates the rule of avoiding multiple casualties with one burst of looter fire for the greater good of better communication.)

Team members who understand better, fight better.

RADIO COMMUNICATIONS

Radio communications, commonly abbreviated to radio "comms," do three essential things:

1. help team members more easily determine each other's status
2. allow further spread of flanking maneuver and enfilade fire
3. allow the use of a distant observation post (OP) for over-watch of a defensive position

Chapter five describes four types of radios available for tactical radio comms: FRS/GMRS, CB, VHF/UHF, and shortwave. It's important to know that all four of these radio types are very easy to monitor by others with similar equipment. Much as e-mail is no more secure than a postcard, portable radios available to private citizens are open lines to those who might wish to overhear whatever you have to say. To achieve disciplined use of the radio, all team members need to learn and practice elemental radio security codes.

The use of radio codes will *not* prevent others from overhearing your tactical communications. It will make it harder for them to make intelligence use of the information. The use of coded radio transmissions requires some initial practice, but once learned, it is natural and automatic. There are four basic elements to using coded radio transmissions:

- ultra-short transmissions
- channel shifting
- alpha-numeric equivalents
- book codes for maximum security

Ultra-Short Transmissions

Brief radio transmissions exchange the most information in the shortest possible time. This makes it hard for someone with a scanner to pick up your transmission and keeps team member concentration where it should be in a tactical application—on the threat. The best example of making it short involves identifying who is sending the transmission and who it is intended for. Never use names ,and forget trucker slang such as, "This is …" and "Over" and "Copy" and "10-4 good buddy."

Number each of your portable units. The number written on the radio is sufficient to identify the operator. With only three units (and at most five) everyone can remember who has what numbered radio. *After the unit numbers are assigned, each team member always uses his assigned numbered radio.* To call a fellow team member, the sender simply keys the "send" switch and transmits the sender's unit number followed by the recipients unit number (e.g., "One … Three," "one" for the sender and "three" for the recipient). The recipient simply responds with his number (e.g., "three") to confirm that he is alert to a transmission about to be sent. After the sender hears this response, he can transmit his message using tactical vocabulary (e.g. "Three enfilade: forty right!").

Channel Shifting

To further confuse hostile ears, change channels during extended transmissions. The purpose of changing channels is to cause anyone using a scanner to miss some (hopefully all) of the remainder of the transmission as they fight through interference to listen in.

It is also important to have a predetermined secondary channel in case the channel you normally use is crowded with other transmissions. For example, any sender can say, "Go to B." to indicate that the transmission will be continued on the secondary channel. Every member of the team should know how to immediately switch to this predetermined channel. Then in another minute, or at the end of the transmission, someone simply says, "Back to A," and everyone should immediately return to the primary channel.

Be sure that all radios are always set to the primary channel when not in actual transmission use. This can easily be confirmed by asking for a "comm check." For example, "Two. Comm check." (Operator 2 is asking for confirmation that all other operators are on the primary channel.) The response would simply be: "Three." (Operator three acknowledges the comm check and confirms he/she is on the primary channel.) Unit 1 would then transmit "One" to also confirm the primary channel.

Whenever a patrol, displacement, or movement to defensive positions happens, and the team is "on comms" (i.e., each has an operable radio), a comm check should be done. If you have radio comms with another survival group or another location, each group or location should have a two-digit identifier number. Your base might be "twenty-one." Their base might be "thirty-six." When you call them on the radio, your transmission would simply be "Twenty-one … Thirty-six." If they are monitoring, they would respond with their number designator.

CODES
Phonetic Codes

The easiest code to use in a tactical environment is called the "phonetic code" (used every day by cops). Let's say you have CB contact with another survival group and in a regular transmission you ask them to send over ammo. Rather than saying "We need ammo," you would use words (usually common names) to spell out the word you are sending. Ammo would be "Adam-Mary-Mary-Ocean." Certainly any cop or person familiar with radio use would know what you are up to, but to a bunch of looters with a stolen scanner, it might just keep them from understanding. Using the numeric identifiers we have already established for the other group, the transmission might go like this (their responses in bold):

"Twenty-one … thirty-six."
"Thirty-six."
"Your copy?" (How are you receiving me?)
"Lincoln, Charles." (for "loud and clear")
"Request follows."
"Ready."
"Adam-Mary-Mary-Ocean."

Adam	John	Sam
Boy	King	Tom
Charles	Lincoln	Union
David	Mary	Victor
Edward	Nora	William
Frank	Ocean	X-ray
George	Paul	Yellow
Henry	Queen	Zebra
Ida	Robert	

The recommended phonetic code words are listed above. Those readers with military experience will recognize many differences. In the military, the phonetic code for the letter *Z* is *Zulu*. The law enforcement word for *Z* is *Zebra*. You can make any changes to the phonetic code you want, just be sure that all members of your team use the same code:

Alpha-Numeric Equivalent Codes

Numbers can be disguised in the same manner by using any ten-letter word in which no letter is used twice. Two common examples are *blackhorse* and *paintbrush*. Each letter of the word corresponds to a number from zero to nine. Using *blackhorse*, the letters and corresponding numbers are: B=1, L=2, A=3, C=4, K=5, H=6, O=7, R=8, S=9, E=0. When you are about to use an alpha-to-number code always signal with an indication like "Numeric B" (for *blackhorse*) so that the recipient will know you are about to send coded numbers and will know which word to use as the decoder (in this case, *blackhorse* is the decoder). Back to our ammo request from your buddies down the road, the remainder of the radio transmission might sound like this: "Nora-Edward-Edward-David, numeric B, Sam-Mary-Mary, times Charles-Edward-Edward" you are telling them you need 400 rounds of 9mm ammunition:

- *Nora-Edward-Edward-David* spells *need*.
- *numeric B* means you are coding numbers using letters and use the word *blackhorse* as the decoder.
- *Sam-Mary-Mary* means 9mm: Using the word *blackhorse*, the letter S corresponds to the number 9. There is no M in *blackhorse*, so in this transmission, *Mary* means the letter M.
- *times Charles-Edward-Edward* means 400 rounds: Again using *blackhorse*, the letter C stands for the number 4 and the letter E stands for the number 0.

The rest of this exchange would be something like this:

Them: "Copy. Stand by." (*Wait until we figure this out.*)
You: "Copy. Standing by." (*Understand. You will get back to us.*)
Them: "Thirty-six ... Twenty-one." (*Making sure you are still on the air.*)
You: "Twenty-one." (*You respond with your identifier.*)
Them: "Can exchange for numeric B, Charles-King times Charles-Edward-Edward."

Can you decipher what their reply was?

- *numeric B* again means coded numbers using letters follow, use the word *blackhorse* as the decoder.
- *Charles-King* means .45: using the word *blackhorse*, the letter C corresponds to the number 4 and the letter K corresponds to the number 5.
- *times Charles-Edward-Edward* means 400 rounds: Again using *blackhorse*, the letter C stands for the number 4 and the letter E stands for the number 0.

They've agreed to give you the 400 rounds of 9mm ammunition you requested in exchange for 400 rounds of .45 ammunition.

Now obviously (I hope it's obvious) you are not going to engage in complicated alpha-numeric radio codes in a direct-contact situation (i.e., when you are facing incoming fire from looters at your fortified residence). Go ahead and calmly say, "Tango's to my left," or "threat to my front. Truck. Five shooters." If the bad boys already know where you are, speak plain English over the air. Just keep your voice calm and your transmissions short.

In a prolonged collapse of traditional law enforcement services, my prediction is that a number of preparedness groups now flying under the radar (and many other spontaneous ones) will take over security in their neighborhoods. They will become known to each other if they have radio comms. Try to arrange common radio procedures as soon as possible to share intel and provide mutual support.

Book Code

Sometimes a written communication is necessary between group members or allied groups. If you must send a message in writing, or you know someone is listening to your radio transmissions, use what is called a "book code" to disguise your written messages. A book code is nothing more than using an identical book on both ends of the transmission to select words you need for your message. The code consists of a series of numbers and commas:

- The first number is the page that has the word, followed by a comma.
- The second number is the line on the page (from the top down) that contains the word, followed by a comma.
- The third number represents the placement of the word (from left to right) in the line.

For example; the page you are now reading in this book is page number 105. If the message was 105, 5, 6, what would the word be? (answer: *looters*) Complete sentences can be easily constructed using this technique. They key is that both ends of the communication must use the same edition of the same book from the same publisher.

WHISTLES

Simple, police-style whistles can be very effective in a low-tech way. In the absence of radio comms, sentries can blast on a whistle sufficient to wake the team if they see something that justifies a general alarm. When coordinating the armed resistance in a fortified structure without radio comms, *Point* can use can use whistle blows to move shooters from one side of the structure to another. Because radio comms are dependent on batteries and hand signals are dependent on line of sight, whistles should be carried as a backup under any circumstances. Develop whistle "codes" and practice them.

 TRAINING EXERCISE

1. Pick a common radio for your team.
2. Practice:
   - transmissions
   - radio codes
   - "go to B"

Objective: Test two-way radio hardware and "comms" technique

12 TACTICAL PRINCIPLES OF STATIC DEFENSE

One of the primary roles of the three-shooter fire team is to provide static defense of a fortified residence. Static defense is the action of securing a fixed site (such as a fortified residence) with sentry rotation and effective defensive fire from secure firing positions if necessary.

This chapter will discuss in detail the seven key tactical principles of static defense:

- Pick a location that is relatively easy to defend.
- Identify likely lines of enemy advance and set traps.
- Use solid-cover fire positions to protect a 360-degree perimeter.
- Identify cover locations within the structure or area that are relatively safe from direct fire.
- Use a standoff observation post/listening post (OP/LP) when tactically advantageous.
- Set up a guard/rest/sleep rotation and stick to it.
- Pick an "Alamo" (or fallback) defensive position and make sure everyone knows where it is.

SELECTING YOUR LOCATION

Chapter eight details the ideal attributes of a fortified residence. The attributes of the home you choose to fortify will play a key role in how successfully the fire team can defend the home. A house in a typical suburban location is almost impossible to defend from a determined mob attack. I say "almost" because unless you bulldoze the neighbor's homes to flat dirt for a defensive perimeter of at least one hundred yards, a single determined antagonist can approach

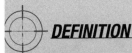

DEFINITION

Static Defense: Securing a fixed site, such as a fortified residence, with sentry rotation and secure firing positions.

through your neighbors' backyards and burn you out with a simple gasoline bomb. You can make good accommodations however with some simple and cheap impediments (see chapter eight).

Practically any rural building or structure with a clear field of fire and a basement would offer infinitely better defensive possibilities. Unfortunately, many otherwise well-prepared individuals and families live in urban and sub-urban locations where they are forced to deal with the inherent tactical limitations of their surroundings. The point is to deal with what your resources provide, stockpile necessary supplies, and make the most effective defensive preparations possible when the need arises.

SETTING TRAPS IN LINES OF ADVANCE

As part of hardening the designated fortified residence well in advance of a disaster, the fire team should walk around the exterior of the residence and identify likely enemy lines of advance through role-playing as looters. In other words, fire team members should ask themselves: *If we were a gang of looters, how would we attack this residence?* Mobs with real-world experience will look for direct routes to your retreat that offer concealment of their advance and a short final rush to your doors and windows. After your team determines the most likely lines of advance, identify good points to set traps and warning devices (see chapter eight).

EXTERNAL SOLID-COVER FIRE POSITIONS

Defensive positions around the fortified residence should have three layers:

1. a core or safe zone
2. a well-defined security perimeter
3. a standoff OP/LP position (if possible)

Ideally, the fire positions should cover all possible enemy lines of advance for a 360-degree circle around the defensive location. This is possible if the fire positions are cited at the opposite corners of the structure to provide fields of fire that overlap. When you contemplate the details of defending a structure, it

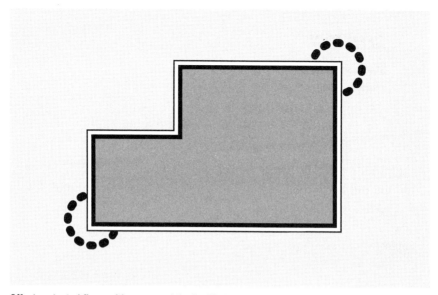

Offset protected fire positions around the fortified residence

should become brutally clear that you need at least three competent shooters to cover all possible lanes of mob advance.

Creating Solid Cover

Although any solid structure that will stop a bullet may constitute cover, in a static defensive situation, sandbags represent the most flexible and effective option in creating fire positions around and within structures. An especially effective use of solid cover is to build covered sandbag emplacements with communication trenches to allow protected movement from the fortified residence to the fire position. Well-sighted sandbag fighting positions and well-placed traps (see chapter eight) can make your fortified residence much easier to defend and, hopefully, look so "hard target" that looters are persuaded to ply their gruesome trade elsewhere.

INTERNAL SOLID COVER LOCATIONS

Sandbags can be used to secure internal areas within the fortified residence or defensive perimeter as well as firing positions on the outside. When the fortified residence is taking fire, it is very comforting to the shooters on the perimeter to know that their families or other dependent persons are in places that can withstand considerable enemy fire. One of these positions should be set up as the treatment area for the wounded. Equip this area with lights and medical supplies. All such havens within the structure or perimeter should

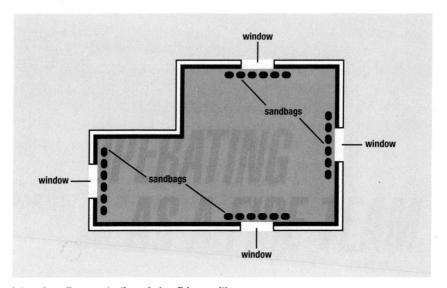

Internal sandbags protecting window firing positions

have water, blankets, and basic first aid supplies. Dependent persons should be trained to enter these shelters within the fortified residence with a command of, "Shelter up!"

OBSERVATION POST/LISTENING POST

Nothing is more shocking to a hostile mob than to receive effective incoming fire from more than one direction, especially if that direction is to their rear. A secure and well-disguised observation post/listening post (OP/LP) positioned 80 to 150 meters out from the perimeter of the fortified residence offers several significant tactical advantages, especially when manned by a precision rifleman. The first advantage is that a sentry in a OP/LP can usually sight an enemy at a much farther distance than a shooter on guard duty inside the defensive perimeter. If the OP/LP is on a hill or otherwise elevated site, it can command a full 360-degree view around the defensive position. The second advantage is that if the precision rifleman holds fire until hostile forces attempt to surround the defensive position, he can take the enemy from the rear. A high-caliber rifle equipped with a telescopic sight is a necessity in the OP/LP, and a suppressed weapon is a tremendous advantage. (Those fortunate enough to live in one of the states where it is legal to own a suppressor should seriously consider one for this specific purpose.)

Use radio communications to connect the remote OP/LP position with the rest of the members in the fortified residence. A more secure mode of communications would likely be a hard-wired magneto-type or voice-powered

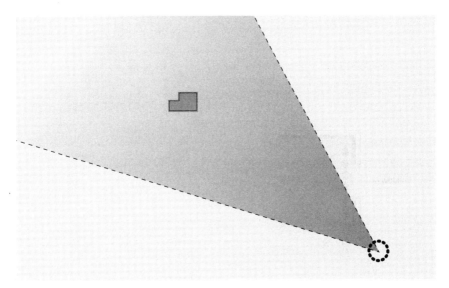

Remote OP/LP position

phone system. Staffing the remote OP/LP can be constant in rotation if you have enough shooters in the fire team, or on a "high risk" basis. The person staffing the OP/LP should not only be an accomplished marksman, but well trained in escape and evasion techniques in case the enemy makes a concerted attempt to overrun the OP/LP.

ESTABLISH A DUTY ROTATION SCHEDULE

No matter what the apparent threat to the fortified residence, the fire team must maintain a 24/7 guard schedule. With a three-shooter fire team, it is possible to set up a regular schedule so that no shooter is on guard duty more than four hours at a time. Pulling "guard duty" means that the fire team member is rucked up (see chapter seven), with his primary weapon slung, and his *only* job is to watch the perimeter for threats and immediately respond to any threats with aimed fire if necessary.

No matter what the apparent threat to the fortified residence, the fire team must maintain a 24/7 guard schedule.

Individuals on guard duty should not participate in any other tasks, nor should they help with any group efforts or assist with any internal emergency. (For example, if the fortified residence catches fire, everyone immediately responds to the fire *except* the single shooter on guard duty.)

Second in importance to a guard-duty schedule is a regular sleep schedule of four hours. Within the fortified residence, create a designated fire team sleep area where fire team members can sleep without distraction during the day or night. A "rest" time can also be used for other tasks at the discretion of the fire team leader. A typical duty rotation might look like this over a twenty-four hour period:

The rotation from guard duty directly to "sleep" is based on physiology. Guard position is very tiring if performed diligently, and an immediate transition to sleep is helpful to refresh the team member. If the fire team consists of five qualified shooters, the schedule can be modified so that the rotation to guard is less frequent.

0000 to 0400 hours	Point on guard. Slack gets sleep. Trail is on rest.
0400 to 0800 hours	Trail on guard. Point gets sleep. Slack is on rest.
0800 to 1200 hours	Slack on guard. Trail gets sleep. Point is on rest.
1200 to 1600 hours	Point on guard. Slack gets sleep. Trail is on rest.
1600 to 2000 hours	Trail on guard. Point gets sleep. Slack is on rest.
2000 to 2400 hours	Slack on guard. Trail gets sleep. Point is on rest.

Role of Guard

The person on guard duty should carry a common police-type whistle on a lanyard to alert the other members of the fire team and dependents to an immediate threat. Regardless of who is on guard, the other shooters in the fire team should have ready access to their primary weapons and combat rucks. These may be kept in a centrally located "ready room" for fast access.

Length of Shifts

The duration of each assignment is flexible to the preferences of the fire team, keeping in mind that four hours is the practical minimum and eight hours the practical maximum length for a shift. But once the fire team determines the shift times, the rotation schedule should be strictly adhered to. Establish the policy that there are no shift trades allowed without approval of *Point*.

Write out the shift schedule and post it at a central location so that all members of the survival group within the fortified residence know the current status of each of the three shooters in the fire team.

Squad Scheduling

If two, three-shooter fire teams guard the same fortified residence (and thus form a squad), both teams can be used simultaneously (i.e., two shooters on guard, two on sleep, and two on rest), or teams can rotate days.

SELECTING A FALLBACK POSITION

No defensive position held by civilian fire teams is bomb proof. It's possible that a mob of looters may throw a homemade explosive on the fortified residence, causing the structure to partially collapse. It's also possible that they could get their hands on serious fire power if they overrun a local National Guard armory. An M2 heavy machine gun can literally chew a fortified residence to dust from a thousand yards out. In responsible defensive planning, a fallback or "Alamo" position should be picked well in advance of any need. Think of it as a secondary or "mini" defensive position. The distance from the primary retreat to the mini defensive positions should be no less than half a mile and no more than two miles. Ideally, a tactical retreat or displacement would be called with the loud command of, "Alamo!" All of the people in the fortified residence (all members of the survival group) would displace in different directions but rally at the Alamo position. The Alamo position should be defensible and hold a hidden cache of additional survival goods and materials.

Evacuation of the fortified residence will be a last-ditch command in a sudden climate of indescribable chaos. It will be a retreat in the face of the gunfire of an armed mob and likely after casualties have been taken. As horrible as this sounds, to avoid a discussion of the tactical considerations in such a displacement would not be responsible. If the "Alamo!" command is given,

Point will be responsible for organizing covering fire as other adults quickly gather the kids and evacuate in the direction ordered by *Point*. This is a tragic situation in which either the elderly and the wounded are left behind or the strong will probably perish defending them. It is possible that bug out bags can be grabbed (see chapter seven) but a hidden cache of emergency supplies at the Alamo location would provide at least a chance at further survival for those who can reach them.

Even a 55-gallon plastic garbage can crammed with emergency supplies and buried at a remote location could constitute an Alamo. The point is, without an Alamo, the survivors after the overrun or burning out of the fortified residence would be limited to the contents of their pockets facing a cold and hostile environment. Alamo equals slim chance. No Alamo equals no chance.

 TRAINING EXERCISE

1. Make a final decision on the structure that will become your team's fortified residence.
2. Have all survival group members contribute to the purchase of a sturdy storage shed.
3. Make an inventory list of fortification materials.
4. Set up a monthly buying schedule until inventory is purchased and stored in the shed.

Objective: Test whether your team is taking this seriously

13   *BASIC PATROL TACTICS*

Although the most likely function of an armed civilian fire team is offering static defense of a hardened residence, it is possible that the residence may need to be abandoned. Therefore, the skill of patrolling should be learned first and then practiced regularly in case your survival group must evacuate the fortified residence. Practicing patrol skills reinforces the team's ability to shoot accurately and comfortably in close proximity to each other. Practice also is an excellent confidence builder.

Conducting a safe and effective patrol is the most basic small-unit combat skill. A patrol is a planned movement with a tactical objective such as:

- cover for dependents (non-fire team members) making a movement on foot
- relocation on foot from one defensive position to another
- assault on a threatening force to preclude an eminent ambush or attack
- reconnaissance to gather intelligence
- regular defensive patrol to secure a large area

Effectively patrolling in a hostile environment is both a science and an art. The science is understanding the many important skills and techniques involved in patrol. The art is a sixth sense about terrain, cover, and the presence of the enemy that develops after one has mastered the skills and techniques of patrol. Many cops who are well skilled in the dynamics of the car stop have been saved by the vague nagging feeling they get that something is not quite right when approaching a vehicle. Cops can't explain how they get the feeling. It just seems to happen because they are so good at the basic skills of vehicle stops that their subconscious is free to process threat cues subliminal to the obvious. Your fire team members can develop this same sense when they become confident and comfortable in the patrol environment. They will become antennas to threatening vibes.

PATROL SKILLS
The specific skills of patrolling are:
- the ability to read terrain features to identify the best route and avoid possible ambush locations
- the ability to navigate a route taking maximum advantage of cover and concealment
- the ability to react immediately to a sudden threat with precision fire
- the ability to displace (retreat) using covering fire
- the ability to properly space ("interval") the team to provide overlapping fields of fire while maintaining line-of-sight contact
- the ability to decide when to flank *Trail* to protect a segment of the advance or engage the enemy with enfilade fire
- the ability to properly space breaks for listening and observing

READING TERRAIN FEATURES
It is very important that *Point* has broad situational awareness that includes the effective analysis of terrain features. A useful skill to cultivate is the "What If" exercise. *Point* should constantly read the terrain and ask the hypothetical question, "If we took fire from that position, I would ...." *Point* should assume that a constant threat environment exists for the entire duration or route of the patrol and determine the route accordingly. This means that whenever team members must cross an open area, *Trail* should be flanked to provide security for the move. Or if a corner must be turned, *Trail* should be flanked to get a clearer observation of the terrain beyond the corner.

Point should always strive to avoid the following tactical mistakes:
- **Sky-Lining**, which is movement of the patrol on a ridge line where team members have open sky to their backs and are very easily observed from great distance
- **Fatal Funnel**, which is putting the team in a situation where flanking is impossible
- **All Open**, which is when all three members of the team are advancing without cover or concealment

To help *Point* avoid these mistakes, any member of the team can halt the team using the proper communications ("comms") technique and express concern about any of these risks.

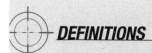 ## DEFINITIONS

High-Ready Position: Holding a gun so the stock is in the shooter's shoulder pocket and the muzzle is just below the shooter's line of sight.

The Rule of 50: A patrol tactic that dictates that In a tight urban or dense wooded environment, intervals of 50 feet (15m) are often the maximum possible to maintain visual contact. In a suburban or open space environment, 50 yards (45m) may be optimal.

COVER AND CONCEALMENT

The tactical use of cover and concealment is a critical element in effective patrol tactics. Whenever possible, *Point* should navigate the patrol so that at least one of the three shooters is behind or within a quick step of solid cover (an obstruction that will stop a bullet). If the patrol must displace under fire, having one shooter providing precision fire from a position of solid cover can make the difference between the survival or extinction of the team.

The use of concealment is always an advantage to the team, but a direct route to the objective is often a compromise between efficient forward progress and use of cover. The minimum tactical cover and concealment criteria for an effective patrol should be the avoidance of sky-lining, fatal funnel, and all open situations.

REACTING WITH PRECISION FIRE

Point must be able to avoid a distant threat by modifying the route or eliminating the threat using precision fire. This presumes that *Point* will hold the primary weapon in high-ready position. In this position, the gun is sometimes called the "third eye," meaning that the muzzle is always pointed in the direction the shooter's eyes are looking. To be ready for precision fire, the shooter needs to hold the gun in a way that requires the absolute minimum movement of the gun to a position of engagement.

Precision fire also assumes the shooter has a solid shooting platform with proper foot position or solid kneeling (better) or prone (best). Most firearms instructors believe a drop from standing to kneeling is the fastest way to transition to a more stable shooting platform.

Maintaining high-ready position while navigating the route is very stressful and should be managed with frequent stops for listening and/or occasional rotation of *Point* assignment.

DISPLACING UNDER COVERING FIRE

Should the patrol come under attack, *Point* must immediately decide whether to:

- eliminate the threat with precision fire
- flank *Trail* for enfilade fire
- displace (retreat) the team using a "leapfrog" or "peel" maneuver

The Leapfrog Displacement Method

If the decision is made to displace the team under covering fire, *Point* must communicate with *Slack* and *Trail* with a yell of, "Covering fire!" and begin the retreat himself. (*Point* does not need to yell "displace" unless *Slack* is outside visual observation distance. *Slack* will stand his ground and offer covering fire until *Point* passes *Slack's* location, then *Slack* will displace. *Trail* will stand fast and offer covering fire until both *Point* and *Slack* pass *Trail's* location. Immediately after *Point* passes the position of cover, he will stand fast and offer covering fire for *Slack* and *Trail*. Leapfrog displacement would continue until the team is beyond the fire of armed assailants.

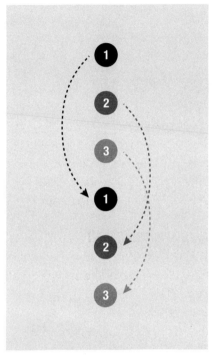

Leapfrog displacement method

The Peel Displacement Method

Another displacement technique is a "peel maneuver" in which the team is facing the direction of threat in a linear formation. *Point* may then shout, "Peel left! (or "peel right" depending on the distance to cover and tactical situation). In a peel, the shooter *farthest* from the indicated direction of the peel:

1. rises from cover or kneeling
2. makes a 180-degree pivot turn to the rear
3. runs behind the line in the direction of cover
4. taps the shoulder of the next shooter in the defensive line to confirm that he is the next to peel
5. runs to cover in bounds

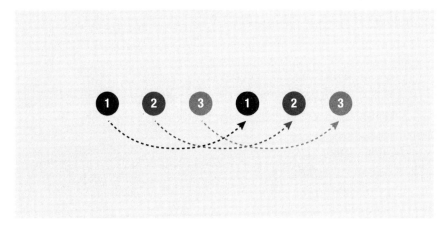

Peel displacement method

The tactical intention of both a peel and a linear displacement is to move the team to a more secure location in bounds until the threat is left far enough behind to resume a regular patrol pace. In a properly executed peel displacement, at least one shooter in the team is giving covering fire at all times.

INTERVAL MOVEMENT

When a fire team is in patrol formation, there is a constant conflict between the need to keep team members in visual contact with each other and the need to keep them spread apart far enough so that they can make use of cover and give effective support fire. It's a delicate balance. Think of this spacing as the "Rule of 50." In a tight urban or dense wooded environment, intervals of 50 feet (15m) are often the maximum possible to maintain visual contact. In a suburban or open-space environment, 50 yards (45m) may be optimal. If radio communications are being used, intervals can be lengthened considerably, especially the critical interval of flanking *Trail*. If *Trail* is equipped with a telescopic sight and a radio-effective interval between himself and other team members, he may be as far as 250 yards (228m).

TRAIL IN FLANK POSITION

In the basic three-shooter fire team, one of the most important tactical maneuvers is to send *Trail* to the right or left (a motion know as flanking) to provide:

- flank security
- covering fire
- better observation of the route ahead
- enfilade fire

To order a flanking movement, *Point* must indicate to *Trail* (the flanker):

- the direction of the flanking movement *Trail* is to take
- the distance out from the axis of advance *Trail* needs to move
- the purpose or the objective of the flanking movement

All team members must constantly remember that if *Point* flanks *Trail* to a position ahead of *Point* on the axis of advance, *Trail temporarily becomes Point* and is then in nominal command of the team until desig-

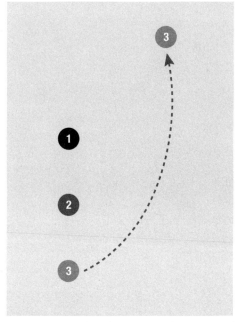

Trail in flank position

nated *Point* exceeds the position of the flanker (designated *Trail*). The applicable rule of small-unit contact is that the person at the head of the patrol is in the best position to see what lies to the front of the patrol and should, therefore, be in command until designated *Point* resumes the front position.

PAUSING TO LISTEN AND OBSERVE THREATS

Sound discloses threats as often as sight. *Point* should frequently pause patrol momentum for listening and observing breaks for three reasons:

1. The pause offers a needed break to relieve the stress and pressures of walking *Point*.
2. A pause offers an opportunity to hear a potential threat prior to the time it becomes an actual threat.
3. A pause can be used as a hydration/carb break.

Point can use two general principles to determine of the frequency of listening breaks in patrol pace:

1. *Point* should call a break whenever he begins to fatigue to the extent that his concentration is affected.
2. *Point* should call a break whenever the route crosses or is about to cross a road, path, habitation, or large open space. Allow time to listen for audible clues to potential threats in the new terrain.

Whenever a listening break is called, all members of the fire team should leave the path or track they are walking and take good cover using sniper veils to disguise their shape. *Point* and *Slack* should spread out as far as line of sight permits to allow triangulation of sounds and provide a broader line-of-sight coverage. Note: *Trail* should still concentrate on threats to the rear of the line of advance because if the team is being followed, the best way to detect that is with a listening break.

Sometimes, a listening break is called not by *Point*, but by sound. If a distant gunshot is heard, the patrol should immediately stop and every member of the patrol grab their compass. Although it is difficult to determine the location or direction of a single distant report, upon a second gunshot, members of the team can get an accurate compass bearing on the sound. Referring to a map and comparing estimated distances and bearings can help the team identify a direction and distance to a presumed threat.

 TRAINING EXERCISE

In a discreet outdoor location, with the team wearing full rucks and web gear but not carrying guns, practice:

1. peel displacement
2. leapfrog displacement
3. bounds
4. drop and rolls

Objective: Are your rucks too bulky?

14 — *TACTICAL ASSAULT TECHNIQUES*

The basic moral imperative of civilian fire teams is to defend their survival supplies and the dependent persons under their protection. Fortunately, it is unlikely that a civilian fire team would have to leave their defensive position at the fortified residence and initiate offensive action, but such contingencies are not without precedent. A fire team may need to assault and retake a base it was forced to evacuate or to make a preemptive strike against a camp of known looters. A preemptive strike might be necessary if a band of looters represents a real and viable threat to the security of the survival retreat. It is very dangerous to leave a hardened residence to make an assault regardless of the justification.

THE 3:1 RULE

In order to mount a successful assault on a well-defended, looter-held position, the attacking force needs to outnumber the defending force by a ratio of not less than three to one. Therefore, the most important practical consideration in contemplating an assault is whether the assaulting force can maintain proper security on its own base, *and* provide sufficient shooters to meet the 3:1 rule. A fire team cannot meet that rule unless it has reliable information on the number of shooters it will be facing as adversaries. This can be determined by long-range observation of the target and careful recording of the number of visible sentries, roving patrols, and/or the number of adult males that are observed in and associated with the target encampment or structure. Such pre-assault reconnaissance is essential to the management of a successful assault. Failure to do reconnaissance means assaulting blind.

COVERING FIRE AND ASSAULT ELEMENTS

Overcoming an enemy defensive position is extremely difficult under the most favorable circumstances. If the target position is surrounded by any margin of open ground and the defenders are well prepared, the attacking force must be divided into two elements: a covering or suppressive fire element and an assault element. The covering fire element uses precision fire to keep defenders away from their firing positions as the assault element rushes the perimeter of the defensive position in bounds, firing from the hip or high-ready position.

Area Saturation Fire

The most basic tactical principle of effective assault is to devote a sufficient number of precision shooters to area saturation or covering fire so that the assault element has a reasonable chance of crossing open ground to the target perimeter. Assume that the defenders will be shooting from solid rests surrounded by cover that will stop a bullet. The area saturation fire element must be sited from equally solid rests with equivalent cover in order to effectively compete with the defenders. The covering fire element of the assault will need to shoot through "holes" no larger than 6" high × 18" wide (15cm × 46cm) in the cover used by the defenders. (This is the typical size of a firing port in a sandbagged emplacement or from a fortified residence.) If the covering fire element cannot shoot through those holes because of unstable shooting

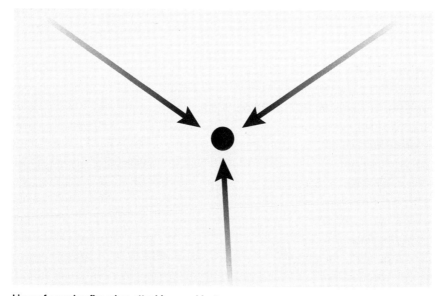

Lines of covering fire when attacking an object

platforms, lack of skill, or lack of will, their suppressive fire will be largely ineffective, and the assault element could lose up to 50 percent of its shooters to aimed defensive fire.

ADDITIONAL TACTICAL CONSIDERATION

There are at least six additional tactical considerations that must be taken into consideration for an assault on a well-defended position to be successful:

- Coordinate lanes of assault with the covering fire element.
- Use concealment techniques to disguise the lanes of assault.
- Use "bounds" to limit the time the assault element is exposed to defensive fire.
- Carry enough magazines (ammunition) to take the perimeter and clear the interior of the structure.
- Carry tools to clear interior obstacles and secure prisoners.
- Prepare a proper medical response for casualties in the assault element.

Coordinating Lanes of Assault

Although it seems patently obvious, careful preplanning needs to take place to ensure that the assault element does not accidently advance through lanes of covering fire intended to protect the assault. At the very least, a detailed drawing of the objective with covering or area suppressive fire lanes clearly delineated needs to be used to coordinate the attack on the objective.

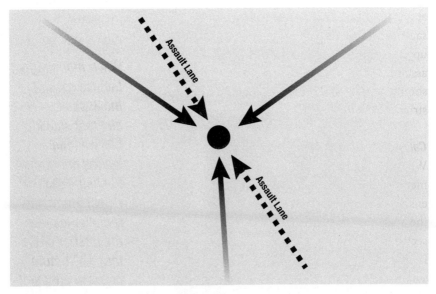

Lanes of assault coordinated with covering fire lines

A sand table model of the target position is best for planning an assault by including terrain features. Lines of covering fire can be marked with colored string from the fire positions to the target. Because covering fire is so critical to the success of the attack, covering fire positions should be picked first and carefully included on the drawing or sand table. Assault lanes should be then chosen based on any apparent weaknesses in defenses, terrain features, and concealment opportunities. The assault lanes should never cross the lines of covering fire.

Concealing Lanes of Assault

Concealment techniques for lanes of assault might include using foliage or irregularities in the terrain surface, or the assaulting force can create their own concealment. Emergency smoke markers (found in boating supply stores) or field-expedient gasoline smoke bombs can be very effective in masking the moves of the assault element. Create your own gasoline smoke bomb by combining finely chopped shards of rubber from tires, shoe soles, latex gloves, or other similar sources with the gasoline. This combination will produce dense black smoke when lit. Pay careful attention to any prevailing winds and throw the smoke bombs so that the blowing smoke emitting from the device conceals the advancing shooters and is not blown away from the shooters.

Moving in Bounds

Bounding maneuvers expose only a portion of the assault force to enemy fire at a time. You'll likely need more than one fire team participating in the assault, in which case, the squad commander can elect to have one fire team up and running at a time, or one-third of the entire assault element up and running. Bounds and drops should appear random to the enemy, but be under strict control by the assault leader.

Carrying Sufficient Amounts of Ammo

When mounting a tactical assault, the assault element should carry enough loaded magazines to ensure that sufficient ammunition remains to clear the interior of the target structure or camp area and secure it. Assuming the final rush to the objective is 50 meters (54 yards) or less and is taken in three successive bounds, it is reasonable to expect that forty rounds of .223 will be fired by each member of

When mounting a tactical assault, the assault element should carry enough loaded magazines to ensure that sufficient ammunition remains to clear the interior of the target structure or camp area and secure it.

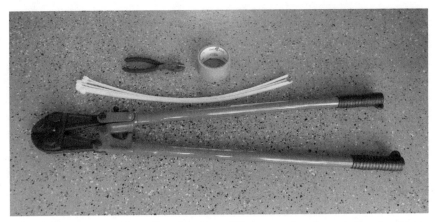

Bolt cutters, wire cutters, flex cuffs and duct tap will help you gain entrance to the assault location and secure prisoners.

the assault element from an AR-style weapon as they rush. (The exact quantity can be determined in advance by rehearsing.) Assume at least three times this amount of ammunition will be expended in taking the interior structure or compound. Also remember that no shooter should ever run "dry," (i.e., run out of ammo) even at the end of a successful assault. Using those guidelines, no less than eight, twenty-round magazines should be taken by each member of the assault element.

Additional Tools Needed

In addition to sufficient ammunition, the assault element must carry tools to clear interior obstacles and secure prisoners. At the minimum, the assault element should carry:

- one set of bolt cutters
- three sets of wire cutters
- ample cable ties or flex cuffs
- one roll of brightly colored duct tape to mark rooms that have been cleared

Interior doors are likely to be reinforced, locked, or blocked. The team may encounter barbed wire or razor wire. Flex cuffs or cable ties can be used to secure captives.

Proper Medical Response

In this narrow application, "casualty" is defined as anyone who is wounded during an event. Estimate at least 30 percent casualties in the assault element even if the attack is successful. Plan for two wounds for each casualty (entry and exit) and have qualified medical responder(s) with the covering fire element ready to come to the aid of casualties in the assault element after the defensive position is overrun. Medical supplies should include not less than:

- 1 stretcher
- 1 emergency tourniquet
- 2 QuickClots and bandage/wrap sets per casualty

When tending to a casualty who has a personal medical kit attached to his gear, *always use the contents of the casualty's kit first*. What to do with enemy casualties is a moral dilemma best determined by the exigencies of the situation, but a general decision should be made prior to the assault so that participants understand what the command decision is. Under extraordinary circumstances of a broad and long-term social collapse, it may simply be impossible to provide medical care for enemy combatants.

PRISONERS

Certainly, the fire team will not be in a position to feed prisoners, nor does it make sense to simply shoo them away without recourse. Do what you need to do, but don't sacrifice your humanity. If you do decide to take a prisoner, follow this initial procedure for your own safety:

1. Keep all prisoners at gunpoint until they are searched and flex-cuffed.
2. Command prisoners to kneel with their hands on the tops of their heads, fingers interlaced. Have them cross their feet (this makes it impossible for them to jump up without "telegraphing" their intentions). Blindfold them.
3. While one member of the team keeps them at gunpoint, another secures their hands behind their backs with flex cuffs (cable ties from the hardware store work just fine). Use two ties, one around one wrist and the other run through the first tie and tight around the second wrist. If you can just squeeze your little finger under the plastic restraint, it is tight enough. No need to cause unnecessary bleeding with cuffs that are too tight. (If you use plastic tie restraints, be sure to have several pairs of diagonal cutters around. Plastic ties are very hard to remove with a knife without injury to the prisoner or the handler.)
4. One at a time with multiple prisoners, help them to their feet and do a thorough pat down for weapons, drugs, and identification documents. Don't miss the groin area on men and women and inside the bra for women. If they physically or verbally resist the search in any way, a short, hard punch to the ribs or ear will regain your control. Do not lose physical command presence with prisoners!

5. Confiscate all weapons, ammunition, and drugs.
6. If you need to move a single prisoner, march the prisoner ahead of you with a tether to the prisoner's flex cuffs. If you have to move multiple prisoners, loop cable ties around their ankles and connect them with rope tight enough that they have to shuffle.
7. If you are going to interrogate prisoners, always separate them for questioning.
8. If they are going to be released, use a black permanent marker to write a prominent capital letter *P* on their cheek and let them know if they show up again you will not be so generous in your treatment. (In the absence of soap and water, the *P* will last quite a while.) In truly desperate times, "branding" can be a more permanent punishment.

SUMMARY

The argument for an off-site assault may at first appear compelling, but it must be viewed in the context of the numerous and complex preparations required to make the attack successful and the likely cost in resources and casualties even when it is successful. When in doubt, stay tight to your defenses, be as low profile as possible, and don't get drawn into somebody else's mess. The Duke of Wellington (no stranger to the horrors of war) said, "The only thing worse than a battle won, is a battle lost."

 ## TRAINING EXERCISE

1. Pick a structure to simulate a looter retreat.
2. Assess assault lanes.
3. Position suppressive fire positions.
4. Estiamte force required to take the position.
5. Carefully diagram the assault.

Objective: Experience the difficulty of a successful assault

15 ADVANCED TACTICAL TECHNIQUES FOR A GUNFIGHT

As I hope has been made clear by this manual, the survival of small groups of people in a fortified residence is far more complicated than it might seem at first contemplation. It should also be obvious by now that *all other preparations rest on the ability of trained shooters to protect the fortified residence with a credible threat of force, if possible, and precision gunfire, if necessary.* Gunfighting is a hard contest with no second place winner. When interviewed, successful gunfight survivors share certain themes with their fellow warriors, and this chapter explores some of these themes.

Although every gunfight is different, certain common principles are generally accepted. (See *Street Survival: Tactics for Armed Encounters* by Ronald Adams, Thomas McTernan, and Charles Remsberg.) This chapter compresses these gunfighting principles into easy-to-remember statements that correspond to important training principles. Be aware that armed encounters are full of shock and nuance, and no book or other academic resource can ever provide a complete guide to surviving a gunfight. The main gunfighting principles we will consider in this chapter are:

- shoot and move
- in a fight—front sight
- fast is slow—smooth is fast
- Miss? Go to knee
- aim low
- Where is his buddy?
- mentally rehearse

GUNFIGHTING TECHNIQUE 1: SHOOT AND MOVE

In a gunfight, the more you move, the harder you are to hit. Even in an armed encounter that takes place over very short distances with no cover, if you take two quick steps to your right every time you fire, you will make yourself a harder (moving) target. You are, in effect, stepping *away* from their fire while *returning* accurate rounds yourself.

> *In a close-range armed encounter with no cover, take two quick steps to your right every time you fire.*

In a close-range armed encounter *with no cover*, take two quick steps to your right every time you fire.

In an outdoor or urban rubble situation, always be aware of cover and concealment locations on all sides of your present position. Move continually from one cover spot to another. At night, the flash created by your gunfire precisely marks your position, so always shoot and move. Practice shooting and reloading on the move. Shoot and move.

GUNFIGHTING TECHNIQUE 2: IN A FIGHT—FRONT SIGHT

When you watch video news coverage of real-life gunfights in far-off lands, carefully watch how the "insurgents" shoot. They don't aim. What you see is area suppression or saturation fire, and it is almost always aimed high. When you see their heads high above the stock of their AKs, their fire will always go high of their line of sight. When you see them dancing around on wobbly legs as they bounce around a building corner and fire off a magazine, you know that any hits they get are pure luck. Fire team members should anticipate that for the most part, the mobs they will face will be equally inept in the skills of precision shooting—and the essential skill of precision shooting is *using the sights*.

With handguns, focus on the front sight is essential for hits (see illustration in chapter three). Although precise data is hard to come by (because it is so embarrassing), most police firearms instructors believe the actual hit-to-miss ratio when law enforcement fires their handguns at specific human targets is between six to ten misses for each hit with an average distance of twenty feet between the cops and the bad guy. During the Vietnam War, reliable data indicates it took fifty thousand rounds expended to achieve one enemy killed in action. That is not a misprint—that is *fifty thousand rounds* for each dead enemy soldier. Fire team members need to do much better than that. *They need to use their sights.*

The term "front sight" in this context also applies to the electronic dot or "scope" that tops the shooter's primary weapon. Put the dot or the crosshairs on the low center mass of the armed adversary and squeeze the trigger. Practice first-shot hits every time you train as a team. In a fight—front sight.

GUNFIGHTING TECHNIQUE 3: FAST IS SLOW—SMOOTH IS FAST

"Fast is slow—smooth is fast." Nobody seems to know who originated that pithy statement or its several close approximations. It could have been William "Wild Bill" Hickok or Jim Cirillo, but it bears as much truth as any six words can to a gunfighter. It is not the first shot that counts … *it's the first lethal hit that counts.* When firearms instructors helped law enforcement switch from revolvers to semi-automatic pistols in the late 1980s, the amount of ammunition carried by the average officer on his or her belt went from eighteen rounds to more than forty rounds. Sounds great right? (The ratio of shots fired to hit took a big dump.) Today, when a rookie on the police training range does a "spray and pray," instructors quietly tell him, "Look, Bubba, in a gunfight, you can't miss fast enough to catch up."

Precision fire stretches your ammo and demoralizes your enemy.

When you train as a fire team, don't compete with each other for who gets off the first shot. Instead, compete with each other on who gets the most first-shot hits. Listen, I'm not saying dawdle. I'm saying be only as quick as you are smooth. Watch each other. Watch who is smoothest in motion, and you will be looking at the best precision gunfighter on the team. Precision fire stretches your ammo and demoralizes your enemy … smooth is fast.

GUNFIGHTING TECHNIQUE 4: MISS? GO TO KNEE

No special operator gets first-shot hits every time, and not everybody in a gunfight gets a second-shot opportunity. To dramatically increase your chances of surviving to deliver an effective follow-up shot, *when in the open, drop immediately to a kneeling position for your second shot.* Dropping to a solid kneeling position does two important things:

1. It makes you appear to be a smaller target to the enemy.
2. It gives you a much more solid shooting platform, which both tightens your shot groups and extends your effective killing range.

When you drop from standing to kneeling, you don't really reduce the amount of vital body structure that is in harm's way, you just compress it. But try this: When you practice with your fire team, have a buddy stand at 50 yards (45m) and then kneel at the same distance. He will look about two-thirds smaller.

This does two things to the enemy: It makes him fire faster, and it makes him fire high, while you duck his shots, and you take better aim.

Firing from a kneeling position is a compromise between exposure and mobility, but takes you one motion closer to prone or to a drop and roll if you are taking fire from more than one direction. So in a gunfight, if you miss on your first shot, drop to a solid kneeling position to continue the fight. Miss? Go to knee.

GUNFIGHTING TECHNIQUE 5: AIM LOW

Cops in departments with a good training budget have access to a terrific video-training device called "FATS" (Firearms Automated Training Systems). It is a video projection system that plays computer-driven scenarios that allow the officer to become experienced in "shoot-don't-shoot" decision-making. The officer uses a pistol identical to their duty weapon that shoots laser pulses, and the screen registers the hits. When rookies first ran the course, firearms instructors like me noticed something very interesting. Because they had also been trained to identify a gun on the bad guy to determine whether shooting them is legally justified, the rookies focused intently on finding the gun. When they initiated or returned fire, their first shots usually went at the gun. This is well explained in terms of its physiology: Where the eyes focus, the aim will tend to follow.

The problem is, unless you are Roy Rogers, it is almost impossible to shoot the gun out of somebody's hand. Because guns are usually aimed from eye-level, most return fire misses because the head is only one-third the width of the torso or hips. Standard, defensive pistol-craft teaches to aim for "center mass," and the targets used at the shooting range reinforce this with concentric circles that radiate from the lower end of the breastbone, which roughly corresponds to the location of the heart. After a lot of trial and error on the FATS system, firearms instructors successfully trained cops to "aim low," and when they did so, they went to consistent lethal hits from the lower chest down to the pelvis. The pelvis is the widest bone mass in the body. Hips move less than shoulders, and any hit that rocks the pelvis should drop the enemy. So in a gunfight, aim low.

GUNFIGHTING TECHNIQUE 6: WHERE IS HIS BUDDY?

Firearms instructors at most police departments teach that after the shooter has hit the target, the shooter should "scan" for additional threats in an arc to the right and left of the (now down) threat. The 30-degree arc of the scan is entirely arbitrary and taught because that arc keeps the shooter from "painting" others on the firing line. If you watch a line of shooters carefully, you quickly observe that the scan is very cursory. Most shooters simply sweep the gun right and left with their eye focusing on the gun, not pieces of cover that could be concealing another enemy. This replication also drills into them *not* to scan beyond 15 or 20 degrees from the first threat. This lazy approach is reinforced because so few ranges allow targets to be engaged in a 360-degree circle of the shooter. So dump this "scan" concept.

I think it is far more realistic to make the student say to himself, "Where is his buddy?" When the shooters think about an armed buddy of the dead bad guy appearing, their visual scan is far more likely to identify pieces of cover that could conceal a man and zoom in it to determine if the cover constitutes a lethal threat. This includes a quick "peek to your six" (a quick look directly behind you without pointing the gun in that direction). If you do detect that his buddy is behind you, take a quick pivot on your strong-side foot and engage the threat.

In a training exercise, I also encourage an immediate move to cover if possible after a simulated kill, or at least a quick drop to kneeling position for all the reasons articulated in the "Miss? Go to Knee" technique.

Fire team training *must* be as close as possible to the likely dynamics of multiple adversaries assaulting your patrol or fortified residence from any point on the 360-degree threat arc. So remember, after you take out the armed looter, ask yourself, "Where is his buddy?"

GUNFIGHTING TECHNIQUE 7: MENTALLY REHEARSE

Detective Jared Reston, veteran SWAT officer for the Jacksonville, Florida Sheriff's Office is a strong believer in integrating mental imagery into your training regimen, and I think he is right on. Create a scene of lethal threat in your imagination, as vividly detailed as you can muster, and imagine yourself prevailing through the smooth and decisive application of precision gunfire.

In public, pick out the most threatening-appearing person in the crowd, and focus on his face. Imagine him drawing a gun and aiming it at you. What would you do? How would you present the weapon? Where would you aim? How many times would you shoot?

From a window in your home, imagine three armed looters making a rush on your front door. Identify: How you would use cover? Who would you take first? How many times would you shoot each subject? Did you make shoot decisions on the lethality of their weapons? Could they use cover and suppressive fire to keep you pinned down? Could you make a quick move and take them from a new position? Good cops are always playing the "If he did this, I would do that" game, but it doesn't really work unless you can see yourself (as in a movie) reacting smoothly, fighting through the pain if hit, and surviving. And always—*always*—imagine yourself winning.

TRAINING EXERCISE

Practice the principles in this chapter at the range under qualified, professional supervision.

Objective: Bring tactics and full-power weapon skills together.

Advanced: Take the team on a guided (tactical) wild pig hunt.

16 HEROIC MEDICAL RESPONSE UNDER PRIMITIVE CONDITIONS

If there was no other option, could you amputate your best friend's rotting leg to save his life? If there was no possibility of help available, could you reset your child's broken bone to restore the use of an arm or leg? Could you probe and remove a projectile from a shallow wound? Thank goodness in normal times we have EMTs, helo-extract, and emergency rooms with trauma surgeons standing by. We have been spoiled by the best medical system that a robust profit motive can provide, but that medical system is much more fragile than most people ever realize. The bottom line is this: If you are reading this book because you want to take a serious look at contingency planning in case of a prolonged disruption of normal support services, you better think hard about how you are going to deal with medical emergencies. If you can't possibly imagine yourself or another member of your fire team performing simple surgery under primitive conditions to save a life, disregard the remainder of this chapter.

In a serious social collapse, hospitals will be, first, overwhelmed by mass casualties, then rendered impotent by running out of fuel for their emergency generators, and finally looted for their drugs. Dedicated doctors and nurses will continue to provide the best care they can in hasty field hospitals, but they will be operating in third-world conditions for weeks and overwhelmed by casualties for months. In a nationwide crisis scenario, they will be overwhelmed by casualties for years.

The greatest risk to a seriously injured person is that bystanders who are quite capable of helping to save their life are frozen into immobility. Coming suddenly upon a serious accident is always shocking and sometimes horrible

(I had to choke down the vomit the first time it happened to me), but you can (first) take a breath, (second) engage your brain, and (third) act. If you can fix a water leak under the bathroom sink, or mend a rip in your parka, or fix a broken tent pole, you can probably save someone's life in the absence of qualified medical professionals as long as you don't panic, and you keep three very simple principles in mind:

- Under primitive conditions, post-injury infection will kill more people than the injury.
- If you just use common sense, you will do more good than harm.
- The human body is a miracle of self-repair. Just give it a hand, and it will do most of the work itself.

If you are serious about using guns to defend a fortified residence, you have to address what guns (and other related trauma) do to the human body. Use a three-step approach:

1. Get first aid training from the Red Cross.
2. Build a medical "jump bag."
3. Collect and carefully read your own library of books on emergency medical procedures.

GET FIRST AID TRAINING

The first step to equipping yourself to give medical aid in crisis situations is to take the standard American Red Cross first aid class. This is an excellent program and so important for regular around-the-house injuries that every fire team member (and their life mates) should take it. Find more information on these courses at www.redcross.org. The only problem with this class is that it is based on the presumption of readily available doctors to take over emergency management. *Do not ask the instructor survival-scenario questions.* They are admonished by their instructors to not answer such questions, and most of them are so conditioned to the status quo that they cannot even imagine the situation you are really training for. Don't turn them off by asking questions they are not allowed to answer anyway!

BUILD A MEDICAL "JUMP BAG"

The next step is to build your medical bag on steroids. The prepackaged kits are okay for the car, but if you are serious about training to do wound management, you need a "jump bag" (loosely based on what a United States Air Force Pararescueman or a Green Beret combat medic would jump with). The normal first aid kits are just too small to add the necessary enhancements. A jump bag is a man-portable bag that will contain all the normal first aid equipment in addition to a surgical kit and suture packs, three times the average amount of sterile pads and bandages, latex gloves, bottles of hydrogen peroxide, Betadine (Povidone-iodine 10 percent), pill containers of analgesics, antibiotics, and other medications. And don't forget to prepare for dental emergencies. A serious tooth infection can easily develop into sepsis without care.

It's important to store a complete set of medical supplies in such a manner that they are portable at all times. You never know when you will need to rapidly displace (retreat) from your fortified residence. Keep a sufficient amount of medical gear in an easily carried package so it is ready to go with you when you need to leave in a hurry. You can store extra supplies of bulky items in shelves or cabinets at the fortified residence, but this supply should be used to restock the jump bag as use depletes the supplies contained in it. Always keep the jump bag fully ready by restocking it as soon as possible after each use.

Jump Bag Options

Select the container you use as a medical jump bag with care. A jumbo camera bag that sits flat and has many accessory pockets is a good choice because of its size and organizational capacity. Another option is a medium-sized waterproof duffle bag as long as you use clearly labeled hard-sided plastic boxes to contain the meds and equipment within the bag. You want a bag that helps you find exactly what you need as soon as you need it. You don't want to waste time riffling through the container or be forced to dump the contents to find what you need. Be sure that whatever bag you use has robust shoulder straps *and* a sturdy handle.

Jump Bag vs PMK

The jump bag does not take the place of the personal medical kits (PMK) fire team members carry at all times on their web gear as part of their combat load (see chapter seven). The jump bag stays at your base of operations unless you must displace. The PMK should always be carried as a critical part of the standard combat load. The purpose of the PMK is to provide just enough emergency supplies to stabilize a serious wound under combat conditions. It should contain:

Israeli compression bandage

Tourniquet that meets military specifications

1 roll sterile gauze

Blood-clotting agent (such as QuickClot)

1 roll compression tape (vet's tape)

1 pair latex gloves

1 pair EMT shears

A jump bag and a PMK

Hemostat

4, 4×4 sterile bandages, nonstick type

1 permanent black marker

Regularly Review the Jump Bag's Contents

It is also important to regularly delve into the jump bag so that the group medic is very familiar with what it contains. At lease every couple of months, I remove the entire contents of my jump bag to check for damaged or broken containers, expired medications, and to ensure the batteries in the lights are still good. I also take a tactile inventory of the instruments and bandages. You never know when you might need to find something in a hurry and in poor lighting. Regularly practicing getting into the bag will save a lot of time and confusion later. The contents of your jump bag should reflect your needs and capacities. For illustration purposes only, the contents of my jump bag are:

General Equipment

Living Ready Pocket Manual First Aid by James Hubbard, M.D., M.P.H., The Survival Doctor

1 pack disposable antibacterial wipes (Wet Ones)

Space blanket

1 small roll duct tape

EMT shears

Small, angled, needle-nose pliers
Headlamp
Small flashlight
Red strobe light (attached to bag's external strap)
Extra batteries for all lights
Light stick
1 permanent black marker
Ten pairs of latex gloves
Stethoscope
1 adult-size and 1 child-size plastic airway
Metal eye cup
Tourniquet
Metal splint
Chemical cold pack
Chemical heat pack
20 fl. oz. mineral oil
4, 50 ml. vodka miniatures
Clinical thermometer
Small tube petroleum jelly (Vaseline)

Surgical Equipment
E-Z Scrub 160 (surgical scrub)
120ml Betadine scrub solution
Disposable 3cc syringe
Metal syringe kit
50ml Lidocaine hydrochloride injection USP, multi-dose vial (must have
    a prescription)
Disposable shaving razor
10-inch angle-head surgical scissors
10-inch straight-pointed surgical scissors
6-inch serrated surgical snips
3 hemostats (surgical clamps)
Large surgical forceps (tweezers)
Small pointed scissors with magnifying lens
1, 9-G large bore surgical needle
Scalpel
4 gut surgical suture packs
4 packs wound closure strips
59ml tincture of Benzoin

16 fl.oz. hydrogen peroxide
5 surgical masks
Rubber bulb syringe

Bandages, Tapes, and Pads

Army wound bandage that meets military specifications (attached to pack strap)
60, 4×4 gauze pads
4, 8×8 Surgipad combine dressings
8 Telfa nonstick pads
4, 4×4 QuickClot emergency dressings
Pack Bloodstopper dressings
Wound-closure strips (Steri-Strips)
4 large tampons
Box adhesive bandages (e.g., BAND-AID brand)
Triangular bandage (arm sling)
Roll, "vet wrap" self-adhering wrap
2 rolls Extra Fast plaster bandage
Roll Transpore plastic tape
Roll 5" × 5 yard Steripack absorbent gauze
2 new cotton washcloths in resealable plastic bags
SAM Splint flexible splint

Medications

Antihistamine (Benadryl)
Anti-diarrhea medicine
Ibuprofen
Acetaminophen with Codeine (must have a prescription)
Enteric-coated salt tablets
Ipecac syrup
Aspirin
Valium (must have prescription)
Cephalexin antibiotic (Keflex, must have a prescription)
Antibacterial ointment (Neosporin)
Oil of cloves

BUILD A SURVIVAL MEDICINE LIBRARY

The third step in earning your merit badge for medical care under exigent circumstances is doing your homework. Not all members of the fire team need to read these resources (although I recommend it), but one member of the fire team must be familiar with them. The essential volumes for the team's medical reference library, listed in suggested order of purchase, are:

- *Living Ready Pocket Manual First Aid* by James Hubbard, M.D., M.P.H., The Survival Doctor
- *Advanced First Aid Afloat* by Peter F. Eastman, M.D. and John M. Levinson, M.D.
- *Tactical Medicine, An Introduction to Law Enforcement Emergency Care* by Ian McDevitt
- *U.S. Army Special Forces Medical Handbook* ST31-91B
- *Emergency War Surgery* (Desert Publications)
- *Emergency Medical Guide* by John Henderson, M.D.
- *Where There Is No Dentist* by Murray Dickson
- *Survive the Coming Nuclear War* by Ronald L. Cruit

If you are serious about being prepared for dealing with profound medical emergencies in a situation where professional medical response is no longer available, the books listed above should be "assigned reading." The very best of the lot is *Living Ready Pocket Manual First Aid*. It is handy-sized but packed with real-world recommendations for dealing with minor to serious medical emergencies. The other references are also important because they can, by virtue of their length, go into much greater detail on individual techniques. Note: A medical dictionary is a handy tool to help navigate some of the recommended references. Dr. Hubbard's book should not be a replacement for the other references, but is an excellent summary in plain language of the basic treatments for the most likely to be encountered emergencies. I keep a copy of his book in my jump bag and recommend you do also. Remember that it may be the team medic that gets hit. You need a ready resource that can press another person into the role of first responder after a quick read of the basics.

FIELD-EXPEDIENT RESPONSES TO BATTLE-RELATED WOUNDS

I am not a medical professional and this is not medical advice. I have carefully read all of the written resources offered, and while on duty, I directly observed qualified EMS personnel stabilize victims for transport many times. I have observed the response of emergency room staff to serious bleeders and observed an amputation in the ER. On mountain climbing and family backpacking adventures I was the team medic and dealt with many issues including cleaning and closing a wound open to the bone. The following material represents my personal distillation of those experiences and that research into primary source material. Be advised:

The recommendations in this section are intended to be used only under the most extreme conditions. Conditions in which the normal EMS (Emergency Medical Services) system has entirely collapsed. Do not use techniques beyond those taught in the basic Red Cross first aid class if EMS remains operational in your area! With EMS operations, to deal with a serious medical emergency:

1. Call 911.
2. Secure the scene from further harm to the injured or injury to those rendering first aid.
3. Use first aid techniques that do not exceed your level of training.

Securing the Scene

Visualize a member of your group being shot or otherwise seriously injured. This is not Sunday in the park. In a prolonged social collapse situation you may be dealing with hostile mobs or the threat of hostile mobs. When your team comes upon a casualty or a team member becomes a casualty, the first thing you must do is *put out security*. You may be forced at any time to protect the scene of the injury with precision fire. Position security behind hard cover some distance from the casualty where they have a good visual on the surroundings. If you are under fire, drag the casualty to cover. If you cannot immediately drag the casualty to cover in the face of enemy fire, leave him and come back for him when it is safe. If you are defending a hardened residence and one of the team goes down, they should be moved to a secure location inside the residence for treatment and replaced with an auxiliary shooter trained in area or suppressive fire.

Initial Survey "A-B-Cs"

After you have secured the scene, remember your "A-B-Cs."

1. **Airway:** Does the injured have an obstructed airway? Inspect for obstructions. Gently reposition the head and jaw to facilitate an airway.
2. **Breathing:** Is the injured person breathing? Give three quick CPR breaths and listen … three and listen … three and listen.
3. **Circulation:** Can you find circulation? Feel for a carotid pulse.

Address Any Bleeding

After your "A-B-Cs," check the entire body for bleeding. The human body carries a lot of blood. It can lose a quart and still fight on, and a quart is a lot of blood. Don't panic when you see blood, just find the worst leak and quickly apply hand pressure on it. Use your bare (weak-side) hand and press as hard as you can. Put your upper-body weight on it. With your strong-side hand, open the victim's PMK and get a Bloodstopper bandage on the wound fast. Keep the pressure on the wound for at least five minutes. If other wounds are present, get a bystander to keep up the pressure on the primary wound, look for others, and repeat the procedure to stop bleeding. If you have a spurting artery, clamp it off with a hemostat and bandage the hemostat in place for transport. These initial steps will probably save a life.

If you slowly remove the pressure from the worst leak and the bleeding starts again, put the pressure back on the wound and try pinching off the blood supply to the wound by pressing on the brachial artery (for an arm wound) or the femoral artery (for a leg wound). If this does not stop the bleeding, you have to consider the use of a tourniquet installed with enough pressure above the wound to stop the bleeding. If you are forced to use a tourniquet, use the black permanent marker to write a letter "T" on the victim's forehead and the time of application. Every hour loosen the tourniquet for ten minutes to provide some circulation to the limb. WARNING! The use of a tourniquet without rapid access to professional medical support may necessitate the eventual amputation of the damaged limb. Use a tourniquet only to protect the victim from immediate death due to massive blood loss. Losing a limb would, for most people, be better than losing one's life.

Explosion or Fall

If the victim was hit by an explosion or injured in a fall, beware of a spine injury that you could make worse by hasty handling. Again, if EMS service is available and the person is not in further danger by remaining where he is, don't attempt to move him. If you must move him, have a partner kneel at the top of the victim's head and gently move the head and neck to a neutral position. Then the partner should protect and stabilize the victim's neck by closing his knees gently around the victim's head and neck. This is a field-improvised cervical collar.

Do your "A-B-Cs" and check for bleeders and broken bones. If the victim is unconscious, you may try to revive him with pain stimulus by pressing with your thumb on his eyebrow, or rubbing with your knuckles vigorously on his breastbone. The victim may become violent when awakened, so be prepared to gently restrain him. When conscious, ask him to wiggle his feet and his hands to confirm he does not have a spinal cord break and ask him, "What happened?" to assess his level of consciousness and mental function.

Broken Bones

If you are dealing with a compound fracture (broken bone ends protruding from the skin), cover the wound with a bandage and use any material at hand to splint the affected limb. Treat the bleeding as described in the "Address any Bleeding" section. If you find a simple fracture (obvious limb out of alignment but no protrusions of bone through the skin), gently return the limb to a normal position using the intact limb as a guide, then splint the broken limb. Whenever you splint a broken bone, be sure not to make the splint so tight that you cut off circulation. Check for blue color or numbness of the fingers and toes on the splinted limb and resplint if necessary.

WOUND MANAGEMENT

When you get the victim back to your base or other secure location and have access to your medical jump bag, you will need to prepare for wound management. This is the most likely time for *you* to introduce an unintended infection that could put the patient at risk. In a social collapse environment so severe that EMS has ceased to function, your fire team medic is now the medical caregiver, and the first and most important rule of wound management is *don't pollute the wound!*

Here is a protocol you may wish to follow to avoid adding infection to injury: Nothing unsanitized touches anything that touches anything that touches the wound. This three-step defensive procedure also helps protect you from any blood-born diseases the patient might have. The following preparations should apply to all persons assisting the fire team medic with wound management.

Nothing unsanitized touches anything that touches anything that touches the wound.

1. Clip fingernails short. Wash hands and forearms vigorously for five minutes with antibacterial soap or Betadine scrub solution.
2. Dry hands with only specially prepared towels that have been handled after washing by people wearing latex gloves, or use paper towels from an unopened roll (completely sealed in their original plastic covers).
3. Medic and assistant(s) don new latex gloves and masks.
4. Boil all instruments for at least twenty minutes and let cool for ten minutes. (Note: Water rusts the edges of metal scissors and scalpels. Add five tablespoons of cooking oil to the boiling water to help avoid this. It won't affect the sterilization process.)
5. Recover the instruments from the water they were boiled in, place them on a sterile towel, and cover with another sterile towel. Save the boiled water in the container it was boiled in.
6. All bandages or pads should remain in their paper containers until used. You will need lots of them.

7. Surgical tools, when in use, may be wiped by an assistant with a clean bandage soaked in alcohol or vodka, but do not cross contaminate from one patient to another.
8. Have a sturdy container available to contain used bandages and wipes. Burn them later, they are hazardous waste.

You are now ready to go to work with sterile tools, wipes and bandages that have only been touched by gloved hands. *Nothing unsanitized touches anything that touches anything that touches the wound.* Paying careful attention to sterile procedures inspires confidence in your skills, which calms the patient and assistants and provides you time to mentally prepare for what you have to do to clean and bandage the wound.

First, remove the bandages that are in place. If they stick to the wound or if the wound is scabbed over, gently soak the bandages and the scab with hydrogen peroxide or rubbing alcohol until the bandages can be easily removed. You must gain physical access to all areas of the wound because you must presume it is contaminated with dirt and debris. Pack the open wound with pads or gauze and vigorously clean all skin surfaces around the wound with Betadine or alcohol. Surround the area of the wound with clean towels, then clean the wound itself by flushing it with liberal applications of sterile water (boiled and cooled). Pour the water directly into the wound from a height of 10 to 12 inches (25cm to 30cm), or flush vigorously with a bulb syringe. Debris embedded in the wound can be removed with the tweezers or brushed to loosen with a new toothbrush (taken directly from its original, sealed plastic container). Continuous light capillary bleeding is to be expected and can be controlled by your assistant using gauze wipes to mop up the water and the bleeding.

You may need to "debride" the wound (remove foreign objects such as dirt or stones and dead tissue). Dead tissue will feel hard and look black. Remove all of it with the pointed scissors or scalpel. After the cleaning and debridement, the wound should look pink and clear of all debris and dead tissue. At that point, cover all surfaces of the wound with a light application of antibacterial cream (Neosporin) and apply fresh bandages. Large or gaping wounds should be packed open. They will need to be drained of fluids and will heal from the bottom up. Pack them with rolls of clean bandage material, lightly soaked in a salt solution (1 teaspoon salt for every quart of boiled water), and lightly cover the entire wound with a thin layer of bandage material to let air in but keep dirt and flies out.

Closing a Wound

On a wound caused by a cut or a puncture, after cleaning and application of antibacterial ointment, shave the skin for an inch around the wound, and carefully

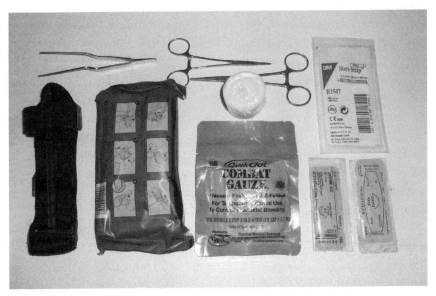

Wound closure equipment

clean that freshly shaved area with alcohol. When the skin around the wound is clean and dry, paint that area with tincture of Benzoin if you have it. Gently bring the skin margins together with your sterile tools and place a wound closure strip (Steri-Strips) across the wound to close the margins. Use as many of these strips as you need to secure the wound. Finally, loosely bandage the wound over the strips to protect it. Shaving and cleaning the skin surface around the margins of the wound and applying the tincture of Benzoin will ensure the wound closure strips get a good hold on both sides of the wound.

Sutures: On high-stress body parts (parts that move a lot), such as the scalp, elbow, hand, or buttock, you may need to suture the wound after cleaning, debridement, and antibiotic ointment. Suturing is a simple process of sewing the wound margins together with a series of loops and a secure knot through the skin layer. It's best to use commercial suture packs, but the medic can make a field-improvised suture kit from dental floss, a fine curved needle, and a pair of needle-nose pliers to hold the needle. If you have a really great relationship with your doctor, get him to teach you how to suture. It is easy to practice on an orange.

Serious wounds will need to be rebandaged many times.

PNEUMOTHORAX

Under battle conditions you may need to deal with a gunshot to the chest that causes air to pass from the lungs through the chest wall. Pneumothorax is an abnormal collection of air in the pleural sack surrounding the lungs that inhibits mechanical respiration. This is commonly referred to as a "sucking chest wound." It is treated in the field by immediately covering the wound opening with something that will prevent the passage of air, like a plastic bag or plastic bandage cover. Bandage as normal. Keep the patient in an elevated seated position if possible. If he complains that he can't get a breath, loosen the bandage to allow air trapped in the pleural sack to be released. That should release the compression on the lungs and ease the effort of breathing. Be sure to check for both an entry and an exit wound that may cause pneumothorax.

PAIN MANAGEMENT

Consult with your doctor to see if he or she is willing to prescribe pain management medication on a "just-in-case" basis.

In the absence of pain meds, you will be performing Civil-War-era medicine. Small wounds can be made easier to suture if you use ice or snow to numb the area. For major procedures, the liberal application of many sips of vodka by mouth can make the pain more manageable for some patients. (A small pre-surgery "tot" won't hurt you either.) Be sure to enquire if the patient is a nasty drunk prior to using this technique and plan accordingly. Don't use aspirin for post-surgery pain management; it inhibits clotting.

SWAT BREATHING

Finally, if you are shot and retain consciousness, you can do something very important to save your own life. You can actually slow your pulse rate and bleeding by doing "SWAT breathing." SWAT breathing involves inhaling slowly through your nose and holding that breath for a slow count of five and then exhaling through your mouth and holding an empty chest for a slow count of five. Repeat and repeat and repeat as necessary until panic subsides. It goes like this:

1. Inhale slowly through your nose.
2. Hold that lung full of air and say silently to yourself … "1 and 2 and 3 and 4 and 5."
3. Slowly exhale the breath through your mouth.
4. With empty lungs, repeat the silent five count.

Treat your own wound and remember, you can take a bullet and still fight on. Get pissed! Win the fight.

SUMMARY

Now that you have read this chapter you will probably want to rethink your med supplies. For most "preppers," one such surgery and wound management event as described here would probably blow their entire stock of bandages, Betadine, Neosporin, hydrogen peroxide, Steri-Strips, and alcohol. Think about it for a minute. At your base, will you be properly stocked for months of being your own doctor? Could you handle at least three such injuries to your team or dependents and still have supplies in reserve? Modify your inventory of medical supplies accordingly.

TRAINING EXERCISE

1. Purchase and thaw a frozen turkey.
2. Firmly mount the turkey to a board or outdoor table.
3. Roughly gouge a ragged wound the size of a tennis ball into one side of the turkey breast.
4. Cut three incisions ½" (13mm) deep and 3" (8cm) long into the opposite side of the turkey breast.
5. Rub dirt and debris into all wounds.
6. Cover all wounds with ketchup and wait one hour.
7. Thoroughly clean, dress, and pack open or suture all wounds.

Objective: Test your "jump bag" and wound management skills.

Advanced: Butcher and cook the turkey over an open fire and eat it.

17 ADVANCED OUTDOOR SKILLS FOR A DISPLACEMENT SCENARIO

Although your family may never need to spend the night away from your fortified residence, in a crisis, you never know when you may need to call an "Alamo" and move to another location. Understanding some advanced outdoor survival techniques could make the difference between a temporary inconvenience and a terminal event as you move from one location to another. Unless you have actually been forced by circumstances to spend the night away from your hunting camp or cabin or car (I have), it's very hard to relate to the experience. It can be a real test of your mental toughness and capacity to make the best of what you've got. Fortunately, the escape and evasion kit contents in your pockets (see chapter seven) and the material in your combat ruck should make a tremendous difference in whether you simply survive the experience or handle it without physical injury or insult to your self-confidence.

Most survival books contain the same basic practical suggestions, but the ones listed below each contain individual gems. A collection dedicated specifically to this topic should include:

- *Everybody's Outdoor Survival Guide* by Don Paul
- *Bushcraft* by Richard Graves
- *The Master Backwoodsman* by Bradford Angier
- *Bushcraft: Outdoor Skills and Wilderness Survival* by Mors Kochanski
- *The Backyard Homestead* by Carleen Madigan
- *Outdoor Survival Skills* by Larry Dean Olsen
- *Build the Perfect Bug Out Bag* by Creek Stewart

To be truly prepared for surviving a disaster (either natural or man-made), there are a number of outdoor skills everyone in your survival group (not just fire team) should master. This chapter gives an overview of these essential skills, but simply reading about them is not enough. You must practice and field-test these skills until you are proficient at them.

FIRE-BUILDING SKILLS

Fire-building skills are at the very top of the list of necessary survival skills. In a post-collapse outdoor survival situation, the psychological comfort of a fire may be very difficult to resist if you are forced to overnight away from a fortified residence. Unfortunately, not only does a campfire make a significant light signature, but the smell of wood smoke is discernible as far away as a half mile from the source if it remains concentrated. To achieve much of the same comfort as a campfire without the threat of exposure, use the fuel tabs from your combat ruck to boil water in your cook set. A cup of tea or coffee, or especially sugary hot chocolate, will make a tremendous impact on your sense of control over your environment.

If you decide that a campfire is tactically justified, there are five things you can do to significantly reduce the dangers of discovery by roving bands of looters:

- Keep an eye on the weather.
- Keep it small.
- Fan it constantly.
- Use a fire trench.
- Build it under a tree.

Work With the Weather

Gusty and shifting winds quickly disperse campfire smoke, thus dramatically reducing the threat of smoke smell giving away your location. And although rain makes it harder to get a fire started, it also dramatically reduces the chances of the fire's light or smoke giving away your position. In a steady rain, rig a rain shelter or roof at least 4 feet (1.2m) above the fire, find dead wood (still on the tree), and use your knife to scrape away the outer damp layer to reveal the dry wood underneath. The fire starters in your kit should ignite small pieces that will, in turn, heat the larger pieces to ignition. Remember that no matter how nasty the conditions, *you must assign someone to area security*. With all the members of your team staring at a fire, their night vision will be compromised leaving them unable to see approaching threats.

Keep the Fire Small

The old Native American wisdom is that a white man builds a big fire and sits way back while a Native American builds a little fire and sits up close. Keep your survival fire as small as possible. Campfires require sufficient heat generation to convert cellulose wood fiber to gas. (It's the gas that actually burns.) Monitor your fire carefully to maintain the minimum heat generation necessary to sustain combustion and no more. This means you will more or less be constantly feeding the fire wood that is small in diameter (no more than 1 inch [2.5cm] thick). Be sure you have gathered enough fuel to sustain the fire before you start it.

Constantly Fan the Fire

If you are in a group, designate one person with no other job but fanning the fire. The more oxygen you feed the fire, the greater the heat output and the less smoke will be generated. Smoke is the by-product of incomplete combustion, usually caused by damp wood. By increasing the oxygen supply, you will decrease the smoke. Fanning the fire can be done with a hat, an empty cardboard rations box, or even better with the 36 inches (91cm) of flexible hose from your ruck. Aim the end of the hose at the base of the fire and blow through it. Never aim at the top of the fire .

Use a Fire Trench

To make a small fire as efficient as possible and dramatically reduce the light signature, dig a fire trench. A fire trench is a straight trench about 6 inches (15cm) wide, by 10 inches (25cm) deep by 5 feet (1.5m) long with gradually sloping ends. The trick is to dig the fire trench in line with the prevailing wind. If the trench walls are firm, your boiling pot can be placed directly over the fire resting on the edges of the trench. In a calm wind situation, if you build your small fire under a pine or fir tree, and keep it fanned, the branches of the tree will help dissipate whatever smoke remains.

SHELTER-MAKING SKILLS

Shelter is vital to protect you from exposure and hypothermia. Outdoor survival books are quite good at describing field-expedient shelters. The problem with most of these shelters is they take a long time to build, and you won't have that much time in a tactical situation. Survival group members should encounter an overnight outdoor sheltering situation only if they are forced to displace from their fortified residence or if they are in transit to it. If children are involved, a small tent is essential for their comfort and feeling of security, which translates into keeping them quiet—a critical tactical consideration.

The most important feature in any overnight position is insulation from the ground. Heat is lost from the body by radiation (i.e., from the skin) and conduction (i.e., contact with a cold surface). Radiation heat loss is reduced by insulated or layered clothing, especially over high radiation areas like the head, hands, feet, and face. In a survival situation, heat loss by conduction is most commonly caused by direct contact with the ground. Always provide insulation, such as leaves or pine boughs, between the sleeping or rest position and the ground, including the floor of a tent. A single layer of plastic will not keep the cold of the ground from penetrating through to your skin.

Establishing a Security Post

During an overnight shelter situation, at least one of the members of the fire team must be on armed security. This guard needs to be in an overwatch position, meaning a position that is away from the tent area but close enough to keep an eye on it. The guard's ruck contains everything he needs to tolerate cold and wet conditions and remain combat effective if he uses the hasty-shelter technique described next.

The "Hasty Shelter"

This shelter technique is a variation of one used during in the frontier days. Critical to the comfort and utility of the hasty shelter is where you place it. Ideally, the area directly to the rear of the hasty shelter should be impenetrable to stealthy looters. In an urban or suburban situation, this might be a structural wall behind the position. In an outdoor setting, this might be an area of very thick brush, a rock face, or a steep incline. The point is that while you are on sentry duty, you don't want to be constantly craning your neck to check out the inevitable little noises behind you. This is especially important if you are using the hasty shelter because every time you move, it will bleed warm air.

An effective hasty shelter position allows you to stay alert without shivering. It requires four elements:

- a comfortable sitting position
- insulation from the ground
- a small heat source
- keeping your primary weapon covered but at the ready

To find a comfortable sitting position, look for a wide tree trunk with a slight angle away from the line of sight or similar structure with a slight angle, such as building debris, a downed tree, or rock face. Make sure that you are actually sitting on something other than the cold ground and leaning on something other than the tree or other brace to avoid conduction heat loss. Natural forest insulation, such as pine boughs or a thick pile of leaves, works adequately for a seat as does scraps of Sheetrock, cardboard, or fiberglass insulation in an urban setting, Tuck your poncho liner behind you and under your

A person in a hasty shelter

butt. After removing what you will need for the overnight from your ruck, you can use it for your seat.

The next step is to turn your poncho into a heated tent that you wear. (In frontier days, they used a thick wool blanket.) This is safely done by sitting cross-legged with a small hole dug between your crossed legs and using a small flame source, such as fuel tabs or Sterno-type canned heat. Even a candle will impart a surprising amount of heat. "Safely" in this context is, of course, a relative term. Plan on getting singed as you learn how to do this. Dig the hole deep enough so that no flame of any kind exceeds its top. Keep your poncho loose enough to allow adequate air entry to feed the fuel source but close enough so that the airspace you need to heat remains small. Tie the neck cord tight because fuel tabs and canned heat both emit toxic fumes when burning. (Your head and face can be protected from the cold by your cap and bandana.)

The poncho is a minitent for your arms, hands, and torso. When you light the fuel source, hold your breath and duck under the poncho so you can see what you are doing under the poncho. Then stick your head back out the opening and cinch it up after ignition. You will not likely have enough fuel to keep such a heat source constantly operating. The capacity to fire it up occasionally will keep you warm enough to stand the sentry duty.

From the sentry position, you must be able to get your primary weapon into action quickly and smoothly. It can be kept along your side under a fold of your poncho or outside the poncho covered with protective fabric or plastic (safety engaged, light source off, of course). Trying to keep the weapon across your lap makes it hard for you to manage your heat source, night-vision device (if you have one), canteen, a protein bar, your radio or comm-cord, and the other little accessories of this uncomfortable but necessary assignment. Especially important is your ability to communicate with other fire team members at the rest position. A regular "tug" on the comm line or breaking radio squelch on the hour is comforting to both the sentry and the shooters at rest.

GATHERING FOOD

Getting food out of the wilderness is a lot tougher than it sounds to city folks. The survival books are filled with instructions on how to set traps made of natural materials or commercial snares to capture small animals, but they neglect to tell you that without scent "bait," setting a trap is almost entirely a waste of time. Animals come to traps because they are drawn to three types of scent—food, females in estrus, or competing males. Commercial trapping supply houses sell such bait and it can be quite effective when combined with well-practiced skills in trap construction. If you do manage to shoot a *male* raccoon, possum, or squirrel (you will know because the testicles are pronounced) and you can harvest the animal's urine (keep the bladder intact until you need the urine), you have good bait for traps. Otherwise, forget about trapping to get food.

The books are also full of praise for the .22 rifle as a "game getter" and, in my experience, this is also far more hype that truth for the average shooter. It is *very* hard to hit a squirrel in the top of a 60-foot (18m) tree with a .22 rifle as any hunter who has ever tried it will readily report. If you are serious about foraging for small game, a tip-down .410 single barrel shotgun is ten times as efficient as a .22 rifle. The tremendous advances in .410 loads after the introduction of the Taurus Judge revolver has made the little .410 much more versatile than it used to be. (In the hands of a capable pre-teen, it can also be a formidable defensive weapon.)

The real secret of using a firearm for foraging for small game is the old poacher's trick of night hunting. *Strictly illegal in normal times*, night hunting is much more effective than daytime hunting because small mammals are far more likely to approach you at night than they are in the light of day. To forage effectively in a strictly survival situation, you must attach a white light to your .410. Any cheap little light will work and you can simply tape it to the barrel near the muzzle. Use the light only when you actually see or hear the game within the effective range of the shotgun, which is about 40 yards (37m). Small game is likely to freeze when the light is first on them, and that is the time to take the shot. Their eyes will brightly reflect the light and offer a perfect aim point.

Fine-shot pellets preserve more edible meat on the animal than high speed .22 bullets, but they may not always generate quick kills. If the raccoon

.410 survival gun

or possum or fox is still struggling after the first hit, you don't need to waste another shot (or make it easier for hostile ears to pinpoint your location) to kill it. Simply step on the chest cavity with enough force to stop mechanical respiration. Not so hard that you crush the rib cage (you will want to save the heart and liver for the stew pot), but hard enough that the lungs cannot expand. The animal will expire in less than a minute by preventing mechanical respiration. Be careful that the animal cannot arc up and bite you in the ankle. Night hunting also works very well on deer but you will probably need to use your primary weapon for a quick and humane kill.

Field Dressing Wild Game

If you are patient and skillful enough to drop some wild game, remember that heat is the enemy of wild meat and the body heat of the dead mammal should be vented immediately after killing by field dressing the game. Field dressing involves making a cut up the gut and removing all entrails south of the diaphragm. Use a stick to prop open the body cavity to vent the body heat.

The easiest way to skin a small animal such as a squirrel or rabbit after field dressing is to chop off the feet but temporarily leave the head and the tail. If you make a circular cut through the hide around the anus and carefully tease back enough skin to get a good grip, you can literally peel the hide off the carcass in one long tug by stepping on the tail and pulling the skin up over the head. When the peeled hide is all the way up to the neck (the head will remain attached) simply chop off the head with the skin attached. You can then open the chest cavity and get at the heart.

Wild birds should be cooked with the skin on because most of the fat is in the skin. Simply pluck the feathers that you can pinch and then singe the tiny furry ones that remain by holding the carcass over a flame. Birds are field dressed in the same way as mammals.

Preserving Wild Game

Wild meat is very lean compared to the hormone-besotted stuff we are used to from the stores. That's good because it's the fat that turns rancid first without preservation. Wild meat, including fish, fowl, or mammals can be preserved using nothing more than bright sunlight. Cut the meat into thin strips and suspend them on wire or on racks made from small thin hardwood sticks. (Not coniferous because it imparts a bitter taste.) If you make the strips thin enough, six hours of direct sunlight on a dry day will turn the wild game to jerky. Using reflective metal or aluminum foil under the rack to reflect the sun back on the meat shortens drying time. Store dried meat in your bandana or other cloth container. Never store it in a plastic bag or it will "sweat."

Field Dressing and Skinning a Deer

If you manage to kill a deer, don't discard the hide. The deer's skin can be easily removed in one piece if you have a small, sharp knife and take your time. It also helps if you hang the carcass from a tree limb by its rear legs (spread with a cut stick). After the skin is removed, dig a smooth pit the same size and shape as a large pot. Line the pit with the deer's skin, hair side down, and anchor the edges of the hide with stones or pegs. Use this lined pit to hold the many small pieces of meat and edible organs such the heart, liver, and kidneys you collect while butchering the meat. Also, much of the deer's fat (which will provide flavor to your cooking) is attached to the underside of its skin.

Using this technique, you can take advantage of every bit of nutrition to make a stew of the small parts the day you kill the deer. You don't need a metal pot because you can fill the basin created by the deer's hide with water and meat parts and bring the whole thing to a boil using round stones you heat in the fire. (Do not use stones that recently have been in water. Steam inside of them could cause them to explode while heating in the fire.) You will need to make tongs out of peeled wood to grab the stones from the fire and put them directly into the water that contains the stew meat. After each stone transfers all of its considerable heat to the liquid, remove it and add a freshly heated stone. Ten round stones the size of baseballs, when well heated in the fire and placed one after the other in the hide-lined basin, will boil the water well enough to heat the small meat pieces and melt the fat attached to the skin. Dip out the results with your canteen cup.

FINDING WATER

Finding water can be the key to survival. Most temperate areas of the United States have ample ground water if you know where to look. Unfortunately, in a major social disruption, thousands of other people will also be looking.

Three important stealthy sources of water are rain, dew, and seeps. Tie the corners of your poncho to sturdy props to create a rain catch that funnels the water directly into a container. Collect dew in the morning by tearing your bandana in half, attaching the pieces to your boots, and walking through the damp grass until the bandanas are saturated. Wring out the sodden pieces into a container, retie them and walk on. You will be amazed how much water you can collect in this manner.

If you spend some time in the woods around your house, don't try to find a spring with bubbling water emitting like a little fountain. Even if you did find one, if the regular mains go down, expect a line of desperate people with buckets and shotguns who also know about that spring. To avoid armed conflict over springs, look instead for "seeps." A seep is a place where water just barely reaches the surface, creating a damp patch of ground. Seeps are much more common than springs. The best way to find a seep is to look for an especially green patch of vegetation or bees. Bees fly straight to water in the mornings and evenings. If you see more than one bee making a "beeline," follow it, and you will eventually find a seep. (Doves are also good pathfinders for seeps.) To harvest water from a seep, simply excavate the seep carefully with the tip of your knife and place a container in the hole to collect the water that will fill in the hole from the seep. The hole will slowly fill with water to create a steady drip.

Water from condensation in the morning or that you directly observe coming from the ground in a seep can be presumed safe for drinking without further treatment. When in doubt, purify.

 ## TRAINING EXERCISE

In a discrete outdoor location, divide the team into four tasks:
1. find a seep
2. build a trench fire
3. demonstrate the use of a poncho minitent
4. boil water

Objective: Test your woodcraft skills

PART 4

OPERATING AS A FIRE TEAM

18 THE MAD MINUTE: DEALING WITH ARMED MOBS

A gun is power. Bullies (addicted to imposing their power on the weak) tend to think of a gun as an ultimate power source that makes them invincible. And armed "bullies" will be invincible in a post-collapse situation as they go from unarmed home to unarmed home pillaging food, alcohol, prescription drugs, and women with no opposition until they reach your house. When the gang of armed looters reaches your fortified residence, the easy pickings they encountered in the past will tempt them to stand around your home, put some rounds through your doors and windows and make demands for your surrender.

Remember that the primary tactical imperative of fire teams is to persuade armed gangs of looters to pick a softer target. You want your fortified residence to appear to be so hard to take that the mob will simply go somewhere else. The "mad minute" is a way to make your fortified residence sound too tough to take on.

A mad minute is a period of time in which the fire team delivers maximum controlled bursts of gunfire in order to deter an assault through an overpowering volume of fire. The theory of a mad minute is that in a threatened assault, the initiative belongs to the assaulters (or ambushers) unless the defenders can suppress that initiative with an overwhelming volume of fire.

The average household with guns will probably contain a repeating shotgun, a .22 rifle, and a semi-automatic pistol. All have a very distinctive sound. A shotgun goes "BLAST" … "BLAST." A .22 rifle goes "POP" … "POP." A pistol goes "BANG, BANG." Street-smart thugs all know those sounds. If a gang of them surrounds your fortified residence, delivers some probing fire to test you and hears those sounds in response, they will know precisely what they are up against, and it will probably not be enough to deter them. In this situation, you want a sound signature that represents fire power so intense that the gang is inclined to move on no matter their numbers or armament.

MAD MINUTE EQUIPMENT

A mad minute requires at least three shooters armed with semi-automatic, magazine-fed rifles/carbines with a minimum caliber of .223. If all three shooters fire two, twenty-round magazines as fast as they can deliver controlled bursts, that is a total of 120 very loud reports in less than thirty seconds.

CONTROLLED BURSTS OF GUN FIRE

Controlled bursts means not just a steady, rhythmic delivery of fire, but a varied pace of:

- one shot
- then two quick shots
- then three quick shots

Then repeat that pattern over and over again (1, 2, 3) until the magazine change. After the magazine change, repeat this pattern again as fast as possible until the second magazine is spent. After the two magazines are expended, another magazine change is immediately performed so that the fire team member is ready to employ precision fire if necessary.

Variation in the pace of fire creates an impression of increased volume of fire. A steady, rhythmic pattern sounds too predictable and is easy to count. Variation in the pace also sounds like actual targets are being engaged.

MAD MINUTE SUCCESS FACTORS

To repeat the intention here, the purpose of the mad minute is not to put down the adversaries (if that happens, it's a bonus). It is to create the sound impression of more guns than you actually have. Mad minute may immediately transition to aimed or suppressive fire if your position is under direct assault during or immediately after the mad minute concludes. If the mad minute works, the mob will evaporate because the volume of fire simply causes them to seek a destructive path of lesser resistance.

A successful mad minute is highly dependent on three factors:

1. Each fire team member must have at least eight twenty-round magazines in his web gear (twelve ten-round magazines in states that don't allow twenty-round magazines).
2. The fire team is shooting from a hardened residence or structure with reinforced firing positions. (See chapter eight.)
3. The fire team has good tactical communications. (See chapter eleven.)

Secure Firing Positions

If the mad minute does not make the mob flee, the team must be prepared to defend the position with aimed fire. Exposing a team member to return fire during the thirty seconds of the mad minute could be very dangerous if the mob has an experienced shooter or two. A secure firing position for each team member is critical so that the forty rapid rounds can be delivered in a stream without exposing the shooter to counter fire. At the very least, a secure firing position should include plywood sheathing on the windows and sandbags or other protection inside the window shooting positions.

Coordinated Start and Cease Fire

A mad minute works best when it starts from three separate firing positions at precisely the same time. This degree of coordination requires both a clear chain of tactical command and good internal communications. *Point* should initiate the mad minute with either radio comms or whistle blasts. But regardless of who makes the command, *all three shooters should start and end at the same time.* To a streetwise opponent, a mad minute coordinated start and end time demonstrates not only massive fire power (scary), but also experienced tactical command (very scary!).

THE MAD MINUTE IN A SUBURBAN SETTING

A mad minute can be an especially useful defensive tactic when the fortified residence, by necessity, is in a suburban environment with other houses in close proximity. We have already discussed the tactical challenges of defense when looters can infiltrate structures close to the fortified residence. If the fortified residence is taking probing fire from adjoining structures, a mad minute can demonstrate that the house-to-house looting technique is too risky to continue.

Appropriate concerns regarding whether the adjoining structures are still occupied by friendly forces should be given, but generally speaking, if you are taking probing rounds, you should probably respond with a mad minute. Mad-minute fire can be judiciously applied by spraying roof lines, yard areas, trees or other areas less likely to shelter cowering neighbors. The tactical objective is massive noise, well-coordinated start and stop times, and a pause to let the mob voluntarily dissipate.

AUXILIARY SHOOTERS

Auxiliary shooters (not members of the fire team) can be very useful in a mad minute if they have well-protected shooting positions and understand the necessity of a coordinated start and end time. However, when adding shooters to the mad minute, consider ammunition conservation. Auxiliary shooters should be trained to place the muzzle of their weapons just outside the window frame or shooting port to maximize the noise of each shot, but keep them positioned behind solid cover.

Noisemakers that simulate explosions can be very useful in the psychological impact of a mad minute. Auxiliary shooters can toss small explosive devices, such as M-80s, from windows to further increase the mad minute's noise signature. To maximize the toss distance and minimize the risk to the user, the explosive device should be duct-taped to a 24-inch (61cm) wooden stick or (better) a similar length rebar stub. Hold the device at arm's length and use a long-tip butane lighter to light the fuse. Use a backhand motion to toss it out of the window or from behind a barricade. This technique should be trained well in advance. Keep kits of pre-taped M-80s and lighters in strategic locations.

NIGHTTIME MAD MINUTES

Anyone who has ever seen a group of AR shooters on the line doing a night qualification knows it is a *very* impressive sight. The flashes of powder unburned in the short tubes blossom into flashes like fireworks every time a round is sent downrange. If a nighttime mad minute is tactically necessary, the gun flashes will reflect from nearby structures, trees, even low clouds. This will only add to the perception of resolve and lethal capacity that a mad minute carries.

TRAINING FOR A MAD MINUTE

When training with your fire team in a safe outdoor location under qualified professional supervision, *Point* should occasionally call for a mad minute and call a direction of fire. The verbal command might be: "Mad minute, right!" Team members should then practice emptying two magazines in rhythmic patterns of one, two, and three rounds with a quick reload in between. (For safety purposes, all members of the fire team should be in line formation with no member downrange to any other member. In a patrol situation, the end of the mad minute should include an immediate reload and a coordinated movement to cover.) Mad minute simulations should be conducted from the fortified residence with shooters counting out the forty rounds verbally.

A mad minute is: massive noise, coordinated start-stop, pause.

TRAINING EXERCISE

1. Post your team to defend your chosen fortified structure.
2. Using *empty* AS "clones," practice a mad minute by counting shots while sighting in on likely looter lanes of advance.
3. 1-2-3 (pause), 1-2 (pause), 1 (pause).
4. Repeat until all shooters finish forty simulated shots.

Objective: Test how long this takes and if the finish time of all shooters is common.

19 RESPONDING TO NEIGHBORS IN NEED

In a prolonged social collapse in an urban or suburban environment, an effective civilian fire team is likely to become the de facto neighborhood authority. It is human nature to seek order and security especially in uncertain times, and a profound disruption of normal routine will produce a plague of anxiety. During the Loma Prieta earthquake in 1989, I watched while groups of neighbors were quickly and spontaneously transformed into effective volunteer search-and-rescue teams. Most of these ad hoc groups were not led by uniformed police or firefighters or skilled Red Cross cadre, but by certain neighbors who immediately demonstrated the two most fundamental qualifications of leadership: They remained calm in the face of chaos, and they had a plan.

**Remain calm.
Have a plan.**

If you and a few carefully selected associates take quiet and prudent precautions just in case a regional catastrophe overwhelms the normal support structures, such as the electrical grid and local law enforcement, you will be demonstrating the same qualifications, and the response of your neighbors is likely to be the same. If you lead, many will be inclined to follow.

In preparation for a long absence of conventional law enforcement, it is relatively easy to plan for the amount of food, water, sanitation, and medical supplies that your survival group will bring to the fortified residence. There are many excellent books on "prepping." However, your team will not be operating in a vacuum. Your neighbors will have needs too, far more urgent because they will not be prepared. This will be compounded greatly by mass denial, shock, then panic.

Following a disaster, your neighbors' survival needs will be far more urgent because they will not be prepared.

Even if all the members of your survival group are psychologically prepared to *never* venture out from your fortified residence, your neighbors are going to soon recognize you are prepared because you will have lights on at night, and they will pick up on the smell of cooking coming from your house. Your fire team should decide well in advance of the dark times how you are going to respond to neighbors in need. This very real scenario is far too important to put off with the thought of dealing with it when the situation arises. The following books can help your team project itself into the implications of long-term disruption of government and commerce:

- *Long-Term Survival in the Coming Dark Age* by James Ballou
- *Self-Reliance During Natural Disasters and Civil Unrest* by George R. Bradford
- *Prepper's Guide to Surviving Natural Disasters* by James D. Nowka
- *Lucifer's Hammer* (a novel) by Larry Niven and Jerry Pournell
- *Patriots* (a novel) by James Wesley Rawles

NEIGHBORS IN DENIAL

Denial (America's favorite coping mechanism) has profound neighborhood implications that *will* affect your fire team. These implications should be considered well in advance of any possible breakdown of traditional law enforcement services, and certain important logistical decisions must be made in advance of the need.

Denial in this context simply means that rather than anticipating a possible need for self-reliance and planning for it, most of your neighbors will deny that any prolonged disruption of the many benefits of civilization could ever occur. In fact, behind your back, many will deride your planning even when those plans might include taking care of them. To understand and identify with your preparations, your neighbors would have to question their own deeply embedded psychological weakness. Psychological weakness that could in dire (but not without precedent) circumstances, lead directly to the deaths of their own children!

PRE-PLAN YOUR SURVIVAL GROUP'S RESPONSE

Your survival group should realistically consider the following contingencies:
- If a neighbor needs emergency medical attention, will we provide it?
- If our neighbors run out of clean water, will we share ours?
- If hungry children show up at our doorstep, will we feed them?
- If a neighbor's daughter is being gang raped, will we send out a patrol to save her?

These seem to be relatively easy yes-or-no choices, but are they? These are scenarios that must be discussed and voted on at your survival group's regular planning meetings. Here are some ground rules for effective meetings. Always end the discussion with a vote. Record the results for future reference and be sure that everyone can and will respect the majority's decision. If you get a sense that some people just can't or won't comply, you may need to consider asking them to leave the group. A willingness to undermine authority is something you want to address and remove from the group well before a disaster strikes. Likewise, if you fundamentally don't agree with key decisions the group has made, you may be better off leaving the group to join a new one. You need to have complete confidence in your fellow survival group members.

It's easier to feed your neighbors than kill them.

Your group could simply determine that you will not, under *any* circumstances, share your food and water with neighbors. And that you would use the threat of force, including lethal force if necessary, to defend your supplies, even if the threat came from people you have known for decades. (Some survival blogs are full of this bravado.) I happen to think that it is easier to feed your neighbors than kill them. Your group may agree, but when faced with the second week of social collapse (about the time all normal food reserves will be depleted), you might decide to provide food and water for neighborhood children; have you really thought that decision through? Can you imagine how fast the word will spread that you have food for children when their parents' have none? Are you prepared for hundreds of children, including children who walk with their parents for miles to get to your retreat? How do you say "no more"? (Feeding cookies to the bear works just fine until you run out of cookies.)

Does that scenario make you reconsider your survival plans? If your retreat is in a rural location, you will have far fewer neighbors to contend with, and they will be much more likely to have made good plans for their own independence. Country folks tend to be much more self-reliant to begin with. If the survival group is going to rally at the most defensible house owned by one of the group members and that home is in an urban or suburban location, your group has made a conscious choice to expose itself to the needs of the neighbors. You need to have a well-thought-through plan for the contingencies of neighborhood needs because logistical planning for these needs begins now, not in after the crisis has struck.

ESTABLISH PROTOCOL FOR PROVIDING AID

I believe it is possible to carve out a middle position that will help your survival group give aid to neighbors without compromising the safety and long-term survivability of your survival group. It involves expanding your cadre to include several selected neighbor families in close proximity to your fortified residence. Including select neighbors can create a buffer zone around your retreat, which can be a significant benefit. However, engaging in mutual aid with your neighbors (i.e., providing them with provision in exchange for them performing neighborhood security duties) should be contemplated only if you have a very clear protocol about how these allies will be used. The following points *might* constitute such a protocol:

- No person outside the immediate families of survival group members enters the group's fortified residence … *ever*! (Temporary exceptions for medical care may be acceptable.)
- Able-bodied men from allied families will be issued long arms (e.g., rifles or shotguns) if they do not possess them, but these men must surrender *all* handguns. (Only fire team members may possess handguns and they will always be armed with them.)
- Rations will be provided on a daily basis to families of neighborhood allies. The rations will consist of 1 cup of dried staples per person per day.

- Water purification equipment will be provided to allied families, but they must search for their own ground water sources.
- In exchange for the rations and water purification equipment, the allied families will agree to be under the direct orders of the survival group at all times.
- Armed members of allied families will be responsible for manning roadblocks or sentry posts 24/7 under the supervision and schedule of the survival group's fire team and must report for all "callouts."
- Regular meetings of all allies will be held to improve unit cohesion, but the consensus decision of the survival group on all matters is final. If this is not acceptable to the allied family, no rations will be issued.
- Refugees to ally families will *not* be automatically included in the ration distribution. (Exceptions can be granted for refugees with special skills, such as a doctor, mechanic, fire fighter, or cop). If the ally family wants to divide their existing ration with refugees, they are welcome to do so.
- Participation in the allied family group requires strict adherence to sanitation and other protocols established by the fire team. (Clean cooking areas must be established and kept well separated from latrines, which must be positioned downslope from water supplies.)
- This is not a democracy. This is a mutual security contract. Neighbors get food and the survival group gets security. If, in the consensus judgment of the survival group, a neighbor violates the contract, the neighbor is out (i.e., no longer receives aid from the group). No exceptions. No appeals.

The surrender of handguns is an act of deference to the authority of the survival group's fire team and prevents allies from turning into adversaries using a concealed weapon. Do not begin by asking for surrender of their handguns; begin by asking for them to declare and bring forward all firearms that they own, then demand the handguns in exchange for the food. The "no handguns" rule also protects the fire team from a disgruntled ally.

This protocol represents a reasonable balance that can add five or six additional adult males armed with shotguns (which your team will need to purchase in advance) to pull guard duty and contribute to a visual deterrent to looters. Use vehicles to create roadblocks and extend the perimeter around the block using fallen trees. This protocol can also calm the apprehensions of survival group members that the group is not abandoning their friends, but it comes at a price. The price is what the additional food supply will cost.

PLANNING PROVISIONS FOR ALLIED NEIGHBORS

The glue that holds the neighborhood allies together will be the food that your group provides to keep them from starving. (Even on these rations they will always be hungry.) The rations are a daily reminder of who runs the show. The daily distribution protocol keeps them understanding who their benefactor is and preserves the authority of the survival group.

If your group wants the option of sharing food with selected neighbors, you will need to purchase and store food not only for all members of the survival group, but for basic sustenance for your neighborhood allies.

The easiest way to provide the greatest quantity of survival rations at the least cost is to store rice, pasta, and cornmeal in bulk containers. Each day's ration can be issued in small resealable plastic bags, one bag per person per day. Be sure to keep a written "ration chart" of who got a bag that day. No "double-dipping."

Inform your neighbors that rice and pasta need to be soaked, then boiled. If you are feeling especially generous, bullion cubes add considerable taste to the rice ration. Add a can of tuna to the rice or pasta ration on a random basis as a special treat. Grow sprouts to provide something fresh.

Rations for Children

A better ration for children is a mixture of equal measures of cornmeal and sugar and a tablespoon of psyllium husk. (Metamucil is an example of a brand name psyllium-husk product.) The recipe is as follows:

- ⅔ cup cornmeal
- ⅙ cup sugar
- 1 heaping spoonful psyllium husk (e.g., Metamucil)

The sugar gives the cornmeal a more palatable taste to children and the psyllium husk bulks up to eight times its dry volume to create the feeling of a full tummy. The cornmeal mix can be boiled as mush or dampened and mixed into batter and fried like a patty.

Purchasing Provisions

If you contemplate *any* food support for neighbors, purchase these "neighborhood rations" based on a plan to feed twenty meals per day (four, five-member families) for ninety days, which means you need the capacity to provide 1,800 1-cup rations.

If the crisis persists, after sixty days, cut the rations in half for another sixty days, which will allow you to feed twenty people for 120 days. By that time, the Darwinian realities of survival living will have reduced the needy population considerably. Remember, you should also purchase and store five extra water-purifying kits for distribution to avoid the other families depleting your stored potable water.

DEALING WITH OUTSIDERS

If you identify allies to enhance your security buffer and feed them, you are under no ethical or practical obligation to feed anyone else. Inform outsiders (at gunpoint if necessary), "We are an established survival group and can only feed our members. You must move on *now!*"

 ## TRAINING EXERCISE

1. Make sample "neighborhood rations" and cook them.
2. Estimate portion size.
3. Multiply portion size times days times people fed.
4. Estimate total purchase price.

Objective: Make rational decisions now about expanding your defensive circle

20 DEALING WITH LAW ENFORCEMENT AND THE NATIONAL GUARD

While a massive disaster is likely to overwhelm the capacity of local law enforcement, it's still possible that your fire team may encounter "cops"—city police, sheriff's deputies, state troopers, U.S. Marshalls, enforcement rangers, border patrol, or FBI agents. All of these officers are *actually on the street every day with a badge and a gun*. The best way to think of law enforcement is in the context of the 90-10 rule, which is:

- 90 percent of all cops, 90 percent of the time, are regular folks who would rather cut you some slack than write a ticket *as long as you* tell the truth, have a clean record, and show some respect for the badge.
- 10 percent of cops hate their jobs and are in a foul mood 90 percent of the time. (They would write their own mother a ticket if given the opportunity.)
- The 90 percent who are regular folks every so often get confronted with horrible situations that temporarily poison their view of mankind in general, and for 10 percent of the time, they are in a foul mood, too. (If you just found the remains of an infant cooked to death in a microwave oven by a crack-head mom, you might be in a bad mood, too.)

So, if you do the math, in a normal (i.e., non-crisis) environment, eight out of ten contacts between law-abiding citizens and law enforcement are likely to be positive if the citizens do their part. But we are not talking about a normal environment, we are talking about a natural disaster or prolonged social collapse that eliminates traditional law enforcement services for an extended period of time. Under those circumstances, the criminal underclass will have open season to rob, loot, murder, and rape with nothing to stop them but armed civilians. Ask any street cop and he or she will tell you *we can't protect you under prolonged disaster circumstances!*

LAW ENFORCEMENT IN A PROLONGED DISASTER

If the electrical power grid goes down for any reason, 911 dispatchers (the real unsung heroes of law enforcement) will probably be relocated to a remote site powered by emergency generators. They will have fuel reserves for about three days of operations. This is important because most street cops don't think of their guns as their primary safety tools. Their first safety device is their radio. Cops on the street know that their shift buddies will bust the bounds of heaven and earth to rush to their aid if they call for cover.

When dispatch goes down, the entire tech-dependent law enforcement system as we have come to know it dies, and your team needs to know precisely when that happens. (A police frequency radio scanner, available at Radio Shack, is an important part of your comms for this exact purpose.) Cops will then be operating without cover and without the ability to be sent to priority calls for service. When that happens, the last semblance of law and order will go dark.

Prison Escapes

It is important to remember that during a prolonged social collapse, corrections officers are not coming to work either. If the corrections officers do not show up for work, the prisoners will eventually find a way to escape. Expect mass escape of prisoners who will operate in well-organized looter gangs. If you live near a big prison and see social collapse coming, bug out fast. Keep in mind that many large state and federal prisons are located in rural areas. Don't assume you are safe just because you are rural. Know your threats.

INTERACTING WITH COPS POST DISASTER

In the gray time between a sudden disaster and the end of police radio dispatch, it is still possible that your civilian fire team (now forted up in one residence) will come in contact with traditional law enforcement on patrol, most likely four cops in a car on the way to some big problem. How the team should relate to law enforcement in a regional crisis is largely determined by the area of the country in which you live. Some regions of the country are pro-law enforcement and some are anti-law enforcement. The best way to tell which area you live in is to watch the public response to an officer killed in the line of duty. If the funeral route is lined with thousands of regular citizens who stand in quiet respect holding American flags, you are in a pro-law enforcement region. If not, you're not. (Pro- and anti-cop regions also tend to correlate almost exactly with politically "blue" and "red" states.)

In a pro-cop region, law enforcement officers will most likely think of a well-prepared civilian fire team as an ally in the preservation of public safety. (They are usually quite comfortable with civilians with concealed carry permits.). If your team is in the open and sees a patrol car, make a show of putting your long guns on the ground, flag down the unit and brief the officers on your forces and your location and ask them if *they* need any assistance.

If you are in an anti-cop area, stay inside, and if the cops come to the door in areas adjacent to the disturbance, hide your guns and don't disclose that you have them if they ask you if you have any. (Under orders from their command structure, police confiscated firearms from innocent citizens and shop owners in areas adjacent to the disturbances during the Watts Riots of 1965, the Los Angeles Riots of 1992, and Hurricane Katrina in 2005.) It is not likely that you will be arrested for lying to the cops because they will no longer have the logistical capacity to process detainees. When the cops still have some units on the street, in an anti-cop area, they will likely think of any armed citizen as a threat and may confiscate any guns they see. Yes, this is unconstitutional, but no cop is going to be prosecuted for the violation of constitutional protections in a crisis environment, and they know it. If you resist them, you may be shot. If you live in a political "blue" state, the best way to protect your team from involuntary disarming is to have a secret stash of extra long guns. If you are in transit to your retreat with your gear and subject to police road blocks, hide the guns as best you can. In your retreat, in the early days of a disaster, keep your guns hidden, keeping only one out for the person on guard duty. After police radio dispatch ceases to function, so will the patrols, and guns can be kept handy in the "ready room."

In a prolonged social collapse, some cops will still try to act like cops. They may flash a badge and expect to take over your team. Be polite. Tell them, "We respect your badge and honor your service, but we have spent months preparing and training, and we will not relinquish authority for this ground. If you want, we can discuss how we can cooperate as allies, but we will not subject ourselves to any external authority." (You may just earn a powerful ally and find a way to incorporate a cop or two in your team.)

THE NATIONAL GUARD

In a regional disaster, the National Guard can be a real lifesaver for individuals who have made zero preparations. The National Guard has the well-developed capacity to:

Following a disaster, the National Guard will not send out a squad to protect your neighborhood.

- quickly protect key installations and resources
- set up and staff field hospitals
- provide clean water and rations to thousands
- establish relocation centers with shelters, food, medical support, and sanitation
- establish detention centers for criminals

What they are *not* going to do is send out a squad to protect your neighborhood.

Forced Relocation

One of the government contingencies during a regional collapse is forced evacuation of certain areas to relocation centers. The rationale of our government benefactors is that because *most* citizens have no preparation for the absence of food, water, and power (an accurate assessment), *all* citizens will be better off where the government can "care for them" in a central location (a very false assessment).

It may be a tough decision whether to comply with a "mandatory relocation" order, especially if your household includes an elderly or handicapped member or several young children. In reality there is no such thing as a "mandatory" order to leave your home. In all the past weather- or fire-related regional disasters, it is almost impossible to find a single example of law enforcement physically dragging a handcuffed person from their home.

If you do decide to follow an order to go to a regional relocation center, remember these rules that are likely to apply:

- no pets
- no weapons
- no privacy and
- no right to return to your home

Once you exit security perimeters, you are not going to be allowed back in until the government authorities deem the area safe. If you are going to a shelter, bring your own soap, flip-flops, toilet paper, and a drinking water cup with your name on it. Keep your valuables and important papers in backpacks that never leave your possession unattended. (Shower on the buddy system—have a trusted person watch your possessions for you while you shower.) For an idea of what living in a relocation center would be like, including a detailed list of what to take with you and how to accommodate lack of privacy, read *Shoestring Survivalism* by Andy James.

Confiscating Supplies

This forced relocation is made even worse by the possibility of an executive order from a state governor making "hoarding" a crime. (Any state governor can impose laws in a "state of emergency" that would never be possible in normal times.) If the storage of food is declared a crime, your stored supplies could be ordered "contributed to the general good," and the National Guard will be tasked with collecting and redistributing the food you have already paid for! This confiscation of private property will likely coincide with forced evacuation to a relocation center. Your team should be, at the very least, aware that these forced government actions might occur and take commonsense precautions. (Separate your stored food and hide some.)

Many people (possibly including your neighbors) who didn't prepare will gladly surrender all of their freedom for a little bit of security, and they will fully support these relocation orders. In fact, some of your neighbors may gladly rat you out as a "hoarder" in a heartbeat to curry favor with the authorities in a post-collapse environment.

ESTABLISH CONNECTIONS BEFORE A DISASTER

Preparation for a natural or civil disaster is not just a matter of bullets, bandages, and beans. Regardless of whether you live in a pro- or anti-law enforcement area, you can make some very important contacts with your local cops with a little effort. Most local law enforcement agencies have civilian academies. These are classes designed for civilians who want to learn more about their local departments. The sessions are interesting and a great way to get to know some local cops. After you graduate, go on a ride-along (cops love to show off).

If you are fortunate enough to live in a state that allows concealed carry permits on request, every concealed carry instructor knows the local cops and can refer you to one for a ride-along. Interestingly, most public safety departments *Attend a civilian academy.* have preppers in their ranks, too. If you can make contact with some of them, you are really inside the game. Exert a little effort here, and it could really pay off for your team in a crunch.

 TRAINING EXERCISE

1. Attend a civilian academy.
2. Ask to be invited as a guest to your local police department range.
3. Do a "ride-along."

Objective: Make friends with somebody who wears a badge and a gun

PARTING SHOTS

The first time I started seriously considering the harsh realities of neighborhood survival without the protection of traditional law enforcement was during the Cuban missile crisis of 1962. I worried again after the Watts Riots in 1965, the Martin Luther King riots in 1968, and the Loma Prieta earthquake in 1989. I paid careful attention during the Los Angeles Riots in 1992, the 9-11 meltdown scare, Hurricane Katrina, and Superstorm Sandy.

Each time, I purchased more books, put away more supplies, improved my gear, and practiced my skills. And guess what? *Nothing bad ever happened to my neighborhood!* Like the drunk driver who staggers away from a terrible traffic accident because he was loose and lucky, the American public seems to waver along a rocky road of equilibrium. Let us hope that the lucky breaks never desert us.

When I joined the thin blue line of law enforcement, I was, at first, relieved to experience the mutual aid capacity local departments had for their neighboring departments. But then I was sobered by the realization that mutual aid is based on a shaky assumption: It only works if the disaster is of limited geographic scope.

The problem is that although the statistical probability of a massive disruptive event is slight, the implications if the event occurs are horrendous because of an important shift in U.S. demographic trends. If you are paying attention, you can't help but observe two converging dynamics: a steady decline in the middle class and a corresponding increase in the entitlement mentality.

The evidence is clear from Hurricane Katrina and Superstorm Sandy. When government does not provide warmth, water, food, and shelter within days, rage is the result. And in both of those cases, massive mutual aid *was* immediately employed.

The positive thing about the media coverage of localized disasters is that intelligent people are becoming more aware of the need to store food, water, and medical supplies, and a preparedness movement is quietly spreading around the country. But, if we're honest about it, those of us with experience in law enforcement must be quick to advise that if a disaster exceeds the capacity of mutual aid to provide neighborhood protection from predation, you are on your own. Thousands of neighborhoods under siege would simply be beyond the capacity of regional law enforcement and outside the charge of the National Guard.

If you must survive without professional law enforcement for weeks, but you are surrounded by the unprepared who will show rage within days, the result is sadly predictable. They will feel they are "entitled" to your supplies.

The time may come in this great country when once again law enforcement is not "them" but it's "us." To prepare for that possibility, get skilled in the elements of disaster preparation. Identify some close friends who could join you in organized resistance to the threat of mob rule, and never forget that line in our national anthem is not a statement, it's a question: "Oh say does that star spangled banner yet wave, o'er the land of the free and the home of the brave?"

APPENDIX

The author has no commercial relationship with any firearms or survival equipment company, distributor or manufacturer. Brand selection is variable. Prices are approximate gun-show values in a normal demand/supply condition. For information purposes only.

LIST A: SAMPLE THREE-SHOOTER FIRE TEAM ARMAMENTS LIST

3 Smith & Wesson MP15, .223 semiautomatic carbines

3 Glock Mod. 19, 9mm

1 Ruger 10-22 rifle, 4× scope, suppressor kit*

3 Airsoft metal AR replicas

2 Aimpointed dot sights

2, 1.5 to 5× Mil-Dot scope (for 1 M&P15 and Ruger)

30, 20-round magazines, .223

12 magazines, 9mm

4 magazines, .22 rimfire

5,000 rounds, .223

2,000 rounds, 9mm

200 rounds, .22 rimfire

Total estimated team budget: $10,000

LIST B: SAMPLE THREE-SHOOTER FIRE TEAM ARMAMENTS LIST, MODEST COST

3 Hi-Point, semiautomatic, 9mm carbines**

3 Airsoft plastic AR-15 replicas

30 Hi-Point 9mm magazines

3 BSA Red Dot sight sets

3,000 rounds, 9mm

Total estimated team budget: $1,500

---

* Requires tax stamp or parts kit stored separate from firearm.

** See "For Budget Conscious Patriots, The Surprising Hi-Point Carbine," by Terry Fries, *S.W.A.T Magazine*, November 2012.

LIST C: CONTENTS OF THE COMBAT RUCK

Fighting Gear
200 rounds of .223 in 10, 20-round boxes
40 rounds, 9mm
50 rounds, .22 rimfire short
Military specifications gun-cleaning kit
Sub-caliber converter, .223 to .22 rimfire
Knife, 5" (13cm), quick-release sheath, attached to left front pack strap
Can, OC spray (pepper spray), attached to pack belt
4 flex cuffs with cutter
Mini-binoculars
Night vision monocular
9mm pistol in holster attached to ruck belt
Vietnam-style sniper veil attached to ruck exterior

Shelter
Military specifications poncho
Military specifications poncho liner
Hammock
Ultralight Ripstop tarp
Military specifications sleeping pad cut to 24" × 50" (61cm × 127cm), roll
   attached to bottom of ruck
Can, Sterno fuel (heats "hasty shelter")

Tools
Multi-tool (fits all gun screws)
Japanese-style Hori Hori knife (curved pruning/digging tool)
Small folding saw
Red light stick
Mini flashlight
100' (30m) nylon "plumbers string"
50' (15m) nylon climbing rope (attached to ruck with carbiner)
100' (30m) paracord
BIC lighter, 50 matches in waterproof container

Navigation/Communication
Military specifications lensatic compass
Regional map

GMRS portable radio
Pocket AM-FM-SW radio
Spare batteries
Small notebook and pen

Food and Water
Military specifications canteen, cup, and stove, attached to pack belt
20 fuel tabs for stove and fire lighting
3 tea bags, 3 hot chocolate packets, 3 instant coffee packets, 6 sugar packets, 3 instant oatmeal packets, 1 small resealable bag minute rice, 1 small resealable bag Ramen, 1 small resealable bag cornmeal, 2 small cans tuna, 1 small can chicken salad, assortment condiment packs, 3 carb bars, all in resealable bag
Spork (combination fork and spoon)

Personal Medical Kit (in separate pouch outside the ruck)
Latex gloves
Military specifications tourniquet
Military specifications compression bandage
EMT shears
QuickClot trauma pack
10, 4×4 bandages
1 roll bandage tape
1 roll compression tape
2 tampons
2 hemostats
Scalpel
1 pack Steri-Strips
10, 200mg ibuprofen
10, 100mg antihistamine
Black permanent marker
Military specifications wound bandage with small QuickClot (attached to chest strap above Tanto for "quick grab")

Comfort Kit (all in a resealable plastic bag)
Small folder, family photos
Minibook *Walden*
Small flask filled with Maker's Mark
2 mini tissue packs

1 bar hotel-size soap
Wool socks in separate resealable plastic bag
100 percent cotton bandana, camo, doubled (21" × 42" [53cm × 107cm])
Bug spray

Total estimated budget: $300

LIST D: CONTENTS OF THE MEDICAL "JUMP BAG"

General Equipment

Living Ready Pocket Manual First Aid by James Hubbard, M.D., M.P.H.,
   The Survival Doctor
1 pack disposable antibacterial wipes
Metal space blanket
Small roll, duct tape
EMT shears
Small, angled, needle-nose pliers
Headlamp
Small flashlight
Small red strobe (attached to exterior bag strap)
Extra batteries for all lights
Black permanent marker
20 pairs latex gloves
Stethoscope
1 adult, 1 child plastic airways
Metal eye cup
Tourniquet
Splint, universal
1 chemical cold pack
5 chemical heat packs
Chemical light stick
20 fl. oz. mineral oil
4, 50ml vodka bottles
Clinical thermometer
Small tube petroleum jelly

Surgical Equipment

E-Z Scrub 160, surgical scrub brush/sponge

120 ml, Betadine scrub solution

Butterfly infusion set

Disposable 3cc syringe

Metal syringe kit

X-ACTO knife and spare blades

Disposable razor

10" (25cm) angle head surgical scissors

10" (25cm) straight pointed surgical scissors

6" (15cm) serrated surgical snips

3, 6" (15cm) hemostat surgical clamps (needle holder)

Large surgical forceps (tweezers)

Small splinter scissors with magnifying lens

1, 9-G, large-bore surgical needle

4 gut suture packs with needles

4 packs, wound closure strips

59ml, Tincture of Benzoin

16 fl. oz. hydrogen peroxide

50ml, Lidocaine hydrochloride injection, USP in multidose vial

Bandages, Tapes, and Pads

Army wound bandage (attached to outside pack strap)

60, 4×4 gauze pads

4, 8×8 Surgipad combine dressings

8 Telfa nonstick pads

4, 4×4 QuickClot emergency dressings

1 pack Bloodstopper expandable wound dressings

4 tampons

1 box adhesive bandages in miscellaneous sizes

Triangular bandage

1 roll vet wrap (self-adhering wrap)

2 rolls athletic-type white tape

1 roll Transpore plastic tape

2 rolls Extra-Fast plaster bandage

1 roll 5" × 5-yard, Steripak absorbent gauze

2 clean cotton wash cloths in plastic resealable bags

SAM Splint flexible splint

Medications (highly dependent on individual needs)
Antihistamine (Benadryl)
Anti-diarrhea medicine (Lomotil)
Ibuprofen
Acetaminophen with Codeine (Tylenol/Codeine)
Enteric-coated salt tablets
Ipecac syrup
Aspirin
Valium
Cephalexin antibiotic (Keflex)
Antibacterial ointment (Neosporin)
Oil of cloves

Total estimated budget: $350

BIBLIOGRAPHY

ABCs of Rifle Shooting by David Watson

Advanced First Aid Afloat by Peter F. Eastman M.D. and John M. Levinson M.D.

The American Shotgun by David F. Butler

At Home in the Woods by Bradford Angier and Vena Angier

Band of Brothers by Stephen E. Ambrose

The Book of Buckskinning (set) by William H. Scurlock

Build the Perfect Bug Out Bag by Creek Stewart

Bushcraft: Outdoor Skills and Wilderness Survival by Mors Kochanski

Bushcraft: The Ultimate Guide to Survival in the Wilderness by Richard Graves

Case Studies in Disaster Preparation and Emergency Management by Nicolas A.
    Valcik and Paul E. Tracy

The Civil War As They Knew It by Pierce G. Fredricks

Combat and Survival (set) edited by H.S. Stuttman, Inc.

The Complete Survival Guide edited by Mark Thiffault

Contact! A Tactical Manual for Post Collapse Survival by Max Velocity

Defensive Handgun Skills by David Fessenden

Disaster Preparation for EMP Attacks and Solar Storms by Arthur T. Bradley

Disaster Preparedness and Management by Michael Beach

Ed McGivern's Book of Fast and Fancy Revolver Shooting by Ed McGivern

Emergency Medical Guide by John Henderson, M.D.

Emergency War Surgery published by Desert Publications

Everybody's Outdoor Survival Guide by Don Paul

Foghorn Outdoors Camper's Companion by Rick Greenspan and Hal Kahn

A Frontier Army Surgeron by Bernard James Byrne

George Nonte's Combat Handguns by George Nonte

Great Livin' in Grubby Times by Don Paul

The Gun Digest Book of the .22 Rimfire by John Lachuk

Gunfight by Adam Winkler

The Gunfighter by Joseph G. Rosa

Gunfighters by Robin May

Guns, Crime and Freedom by Wayne LaPierre

Handgun Training for Personal Protection by Richard Mann

Hobby Gunsmithing by Ralph T. Walker

The Home Schooled Shootist-Training to Fight With A Carbine by Joe Nobody
How To Be Your Own Doctor (Sometimes) by Keith W. Sehnert, M.D.
Killer Weather: Stories of Great Disasters by Howard Everett Smith
Living Ready Pocket Manual First Aid by James Hubbard, M.D., M.P.H.
Long-Term Survival in the Coming Dark Age by James Ballou
Lucifer's Hammer by Larry Niven and Jerry Pournelle
Manna: Foods of the Frontier by Gertrude Harris
Military History: The Definitive Visual Guide to the Objects of Warfare by D.K. Publishing
The Modern Rifle by Jim Carmichel
Mountain Man Crafts and Skills by David Montgomery
No Second Place Winner by Bill Jordan
Outdoor Survival Skills by Larry Dean Olsen
The People's Pharmacy Quick and Handy Home Remedies by Joe and Terry Graedon
Plowshares into Swords by Louis Awerbach
The Ranger Digest (set) by Rick R. Tscherne
Self-Reliance During Natural Disasters and Civil Unrest by George R. Bradford
Sixguns by Elmer Keith
Sniper-Counter Sniper by Mark V. Lonsdale
Stopping Power by Evan P. Marshall and Edwin J. Sanow
Street Survival: Tactics for Armed Encounters by Ronald J. Adams, Thomas A. McTernan and Charles Remsberg
StressFire, Vol. 1: Gunfighting for Police by Massad F Ayoob
StressFire II: Advanced Combat Shotgun by Massad F. Ayoob
Survival Guns by Mel Tappan
Survive the Coming Nuclear War by Ronald L. Cruit, M.D.
The Tactical Edge: Surviving High-Risk Patrol by Charles Remsburg
Tactical Medicine by Ian McDevitt
21st-Century Stopping Power by Matthew Campbell
Triggernometry: A Gallery of Gunfighters by Eugene Cunningham
U.S. Army Ranger Handbook SH 21-76
U.S. Army Special Forces Medical Handbook by U.S. Army Institute
Vigilante! The Story of Americans, Then & Now, Guarding Each Other by William E. Burrows
When All Hell Breaks Loose Cody Lundin
Where There is no Dentist by Murray Dickson
The Worst-Case Scenario Survival Handbook by Joshua Piven and David Borgenicht

GLOSSARY

ABCs: Initial assessment of accident victim: Airway, Breathing, Circulation.

AD: Accidental discharge of a firearm caused by tensing of major muscle groups with mechanical safety off and trigger finger inside the trigger guard.

Airsoft: Fancy BB guns that simulate combat weapons.

Alamo: A fallback position in case the primary defensive position is overrun.

All open: When all members of the fire team are exposed to enemy fire.

Alpha-numeric code: Substituting letters for numbers.

Ask-tell-take: Asking for compliance, demanding compliance, gaining compliance through physical force.

Assault element: A dedicated group assigned to move and attack a defended structure.

Auxiliary shooters: Shooters who have basic familiarity with firearms but not advanced fire team training.

BBC: British Broadcasting Corporation—a highly credible source for world news accessible by shortwave radio.

Beeline: Following bees to a source of open water.

Betadine (Povidone-iodine, 10 percent): Powerful disinfectant used in wound management.

Bird netting: Black plastic sheets of tiny squares. An impediment invisible at night.

Body armor: Kevlar with or without trauma plates worn to protect body core.

Bounds: Short rushes from one cover position to another.

Breaching tools: Devices such as heavy hammers or bars to break down impediments to an assault.

Buffer zone: A relatively secure area around the hardened residence.

Bug out bag: "Bob" (slang), the combat ruck for fire team members, a large backpack for dependent persons that carries enough basic gear for survival away from the fortified residence.

Caltrops: Small metal devices that project a sharpened tip upward to flatten tires and cause injury to assaulting looters.

Civilian academies: Classes for civilians put on by local police/sheriff's departments designed to make police operations more known to the public.

Civilian fire team: A group of three to five experienced shooters who are willing and able to use firearms in closely coordinated action to defend a fortified residence in case of the prolonged absence of traditional law enforcement services.

Closed wound treatment: Closing a shallow wound with strips or sutures after cleaning/debridement.

Comm check: Assuring effective radio communications between all members of the fire team.

Combat load: The unit-standard gear carried by each fire team member when on duty.

Combat ruck: "Rucksack" (European word for backpack) designed to carry enough support for at least twenty-four hours of combat operations.

Command element: The fire team that includes an overall incident commander when more than one fire team is in contact with armed looters.

Command presence: The projection of the capacity and will to use whatever force the situation demands if voluntary compliance with orders is not achieved.

Common platform: Firearms of identical type, caliber, and mechanical function to allow common magazines to be used.

Compound fracture: A broken bone with ends protruding through the skin.

Comms: Abbreviation for radio communications.

Concealment: A structure or material that masks the physical presence of a shooter but is not composed of material capable of stopping incoming rounds.

Cover: A structure or material capable of stopping incoming rounds.

Covered fire positions: Secure firing positions protected by earth berms, sandbags, or other materials sufficient to stop a bullet.

Covering fire element: A dedicated group assigned to provide covering fire on an assault.

Covering fire: Rapidly delivered high volume of fire into an enemy area designed to prevent them from aiming at the fire team. (See *saturation fire*.)

CQB: "Close Quarters Battle," the study of armed combat at distances of 5 to 150 feet (1.5m to 46m).

Credible threat: An order by defenders to looters to disburse, backed up by the clear capacity and intention to use lethal force if they do not.

Debridement: The removal of embedded dirt, grit, or dead tissue from a wound by flushing and/or brushing with sterile liquid and equipment.

Decoy: A fake trap designed to increase the appearance of hardening of the residence.

Defensive application: Use of the fire team to protect a hardened defensive position.

Dirty dust: The product of a limited nuclear event. Radioactive particles that precipitate from the air.

Displacement with covering fire: A tactical retreat where one member of the team is always providing covering fire.

Dosimeter: A device that measures background radiation levels.

E&E kit: "Escape and evasion" equipment carried in the pockets.

Ebola: A highly contagious fatal disease (example of a pandemic).

Enfilade fire: Stealthy movement to the flanks (exposed side) of an enemy position and engaging them with gunfire.

Farmsteads: Historical reference to pioneer cabins.

Fatal funnel: When all members of the fire team are in a small space subject to enemy fire from various directions.

FATS: (Firearms Automated Training Systems) An automated shooting training system that uses laser designators to mark hits. Trains cops in "shoot-don't-shoot" scenarios.

FEMA: Federal Emergency Management Agency, government agency charged with overall management of disasters.

Field expedient: Spontaneous development of resources or tactics based on immediate needs using whatever materials are at hand.

Fire and maneuver: The ability to effectively engage armed looters with aimed fire while moving from one cover position to another.

Fire team: Three to five well-trained shooters acting in closely coordinated defensive action with firearms.

Fire trench: A long narrow trench dug in the ground to reduce the light signature of an outdoor fire.

Firing positions: Covered areas where precision defensive fire can be delivered with relative protection to the fire team member.

Flank: "Side," as in the side of the formation or around the line of advance.

Flanking fire: Firing upon an enemy from the side of their position (see *enfilade fire*.)

Flanking *Trait*: Sending the last shooter in line to the right or left for better observation of terrain in the direction of advance or to engage the enemy with precision fire.

Flex cuffs: (Zip-ties) Nylon strips used as hand and leg restraints for prisoners.

Fortified residence or home: A structure that can provide shelter for several family units and is modified to provide enhanced resistance to mob attack. (See chapter eight for more information on how to select and outfit a fortified residence.)

Hand signals: Communication technique between fire team members.

Hard cover: A structure or material capable of stopping incoming rounds.

Hard target: A target (structure or defensive position) that is well defended or protected with effective shooting positions.

Hasty shelter: A quickly established overnight shelter using only a poncho and a small heat source.

High-ready position: Positioning a gun so the stock is in the shooter's shoulder pocket and the muzzle is just below the shooter's line of sight.

Hydrogen peroxide: Liquid used to remove scabs and assist in wound management.

Impediments: Physical barriers to looter assault.

Incident commander: A single person identified to be in tactical command of a squad.

Indexed trigger finger: Keeping the trigger finger straight along the frame of the weapon and not inside the trigger guard until a specific target is engaged.

Inert cartridges: Cartridges without powder or live primer to simulate loading, firing, and unloading for training purposes.

Intervals: The proper tactical spacing of fire team members in patrol formation designed to maintain visual contact but not so close as to expose more than one person to a burst of enemy fire.

Jump bag: A large first aid equipment container with handles and shoulder strap. Must be large enough to contain wound-management equipment.

Killing range: The distance at which the shooter and weapon can consistently hit the center mass of an assailant or attacker.

Line of advance: The general direction of a patrol or tactical movement.

Lanes of assault: Approaches to a structure or area to be attacked that does not expose attackers to the fire of the covering element.

Leadership: Demonstration of calm reactions, clear communications skills, physical and mental toughness, and respect for the opinions of others.

Lethal force: The effective use of firearms and/or field-expedient traps and explosive devices that may result in the death of armed looters.

Lidocaine: A topical anesthetic injected around a wound to allow painless suturing.

Light signature: Ambient light that can be identified by an enemy.

Limited nuclear event: A localized nuclear event caused by power plant catastrophic failure or terrorist explosion of a man-portable nuclear device.

Mad minute: The coordinated fire of three shooters of up to forty rounds per shooter as fast as controlled bursts can be delivered. The effect of a "mad minute" is primarily psychological.

Mag change: The replacement of an empty magazine with a full one. Should be accompanied by a shout of "Magazine!" or "Reload!"

Mechanical safety: The safety lever of a weapon that blocks the firing pin.

Muzzle safe: Keeping the muzzle of the weapon from passing across other shooters or body parts of shooter.

National Guard: Citizen soldiers, under the control of the state governor, who can be mobilized to deal with emergencies within the state in which they are chartered.

Night hunting: Using lights to hunt animals at night under survival poaching situations. (This is illegal, so it should only be used for survival following a social collapse.)

Noisemakers: Devices designed to alert sentries to looter penetration or intimate assaulters with the impression of high-volume defensive fire.

Open wound treatment: When deep wounds are packed with rolls of sterile bandage material and not closed by strips or sutures.

Overlapping fields of fire: Positioning shooters so that all lanes of looter advance are covered by precision defensive fire.

Pandemic: A highly contagious and rapidly expanding fatal disease spreading over a broad (multi-continent) area.

Paramilitary: Similar to military in tactics, equipment, and image.

Patrol: A coordinated movement outside of the hardened defensive position.

Peel: A coordinated movement to the flanks in which fire team members cross behind other team members who are providing covering fire for the movement.

Physical barriers (to nuclear fallout): Plastic sheets secured with duct tape to inhibit the penetration of dirty dust into "safe" areas inside the hardened residence.

Pneumothorax (closed): An open passageway for air into the sack surrounding the lungs inhibiting mechanical respiration (usually caused by a broken rib).

Pneumothorax (open): A chest wall penetration injury that allows air to enter the sack around the lung inhibiting or preventing mechanical respiration.

Point: The lead shooter in a patrol formation and agreed leader of the fire team.

Precision fire: Carefully aimed fire to engage a specific target.

Prevailing wind: The usual wind pattern. (Used to estimate nuclear fallout distribution pattern.)

QuickClot: A blood coagulant impregnated bandage.

Relocation bag: A large (duffle bag) size carrier designed to contain basic tools and equipment to relocate the group to another fortified position.

Relocation centers: Areas where the National Guard provides basic shelter, security, and medical support in exchange for individual rights of privacy, security, and mobility.

Rover: A fire team member who moves from one position of cover within a hardened residence to another based on where they can be most effective in using precision fire to repel a looter assault.

Rule of 3 to 1: It takes three times the number of defenders to successfully combat-assault a well protected defensive position.

Rule of 50: A patrol tactic that dictates that in a tight urban or dense wooded environment, intervals of 50 feet (15m) are often the maximum possible to maintain visual contact. In a suburban or open space environment, 50 yards (46m) may be optimal.

Sand table: A replica of a structure or area to be attacked used for training or briefing purposes.

Saturation fire: Rapidly delivered high volume of fire into a specific area designed to prevent accurate return fire. (See *covering fire*.)

Scan: Checking the scene to identify additional threats after the initial threat is neutralized.

Scent bait: Chemical simulations of mammal urine that attracts animals to traps.

Secure firing position: A firing position well-protected with sandbags or other solid cover that allows effective aimed fire with minimum exposure of the defender.

Seep: Where underground water barely reaches the surface. Suitable to harvest for drinking purposes.

Sentry schedule: A written list describing the rotation of fire team members as sentries.

Sheathing: Plywood covers over windows and doors.

Shooting platform: Positioning the body to provide the most stable anchor for precision shooting.

Signals: Electronic or mechanical devices that alert defenders to the presence of looters making a stealthy assault on the hardened residence.

Simple fracture: A broken bone with ends contained within the musculature.

Simunitions: Nonlethal cartridges that function in standard firearms.

Sky-lining: Traveling on the top of a ridgeline or hill with open sky behind the fire team member.

Slack: The second shooter in a patrol formation and second in command of the fire team.

Sniper veil: A net fabric in muted colors worn over the head to disguise the shape of the shooter.

Social collapse: The destruction of normal social relations including civil standards of behavior and elimination of traditional law enforcement services characterized by mass rioting and looting.

Soft target: A target (structure or defensive position) that is not well defended or protected with effective shooting positions.

Sonic alarm: A noisemaker activated by trip wire or sensor to alert sentries to a stealthy assault on the hardened residence.

SOPs: Standard Operating Procedures. A written list of tactics and activities common to the fire team, kept where they are an easy reference.

Squad: A large group of allied shooters divided into fire teams under a single tactical commander.

Standoff position: A defensive firing position at some distance from the hardened residence to allow better observation of threats and effective flanking fire.

Static defense: Securing a fixed site, such as a fortified residence, with sentry rotation and secure firing positions.

Stealthy patrol: Quiet movement of the fire team.

Sterile: Not contaminated by germs.

Sterile wound management: Making sure that nothing unsanitary touches anything that touches anything that touches the wound.

Strategic: Decisions related to long-term issues or general practices.

Sub-caliber firearms: Firearms identical to the standard duty weapon that fire .22 rimfire ammunition.

Sunlight preservation: Using bright sunlight to preserve (dry) thin strips of meat, fish, or vegetables.

Suturing: Closing a wound with a series of thread loops and knots sewn through the skin margins.

Sven Saw: A small folding saw for shelter construction and firewood gathering.

SWAT breathing: A slow and rhythmic pattern of inspiration and exhalation that calms the patient and reduces the respiration/heart rate and resulting blood loss.

SWAT: Police special weapons and tactics teams.

Sweeping (also called Painting): Allowing the muzzle of your gun to pass across the body of another fire team member who is downrange from you.

Sympathetic muscle response: Accidental discharge of a firearm caused by general muscle contraction in response to a sudden stimuli that causes a finger inside the trigger guard to jerk the trigger in reflex action.

Systems of carriage: Pockets, web gear, and combat ruck.

Tactical assault: Attacking a position or group with coordinated force, a good plan, and clearly designated leadership.

Tactical: Decisions made in direct contact with adversaries or in anticipation of that contact.

Talk-it-over: A meeting between fire team members while on patrol. It's indicated by a hand signal.

Tangle-foot: Stakes and wire string at ankle height to trip looters assaulting the hardened residence.

Terrain features: Variations in natural physical terrain aspects, such as hills, streams, gullies, washouts, and cliffs.

Thigh pouches: Equipment carriers suspended from the belt and attached to the thigh with a loop strap.

Three-step sterile procedure: Making sure that nothing unsanitary touches anything that touches anything that touches the wound. (See chapter sixteen for a complete explanation.)

Through-and-through: A bullet wound with an entry and corresponding exit wound.

Tiger pit: A large hole in the ground, with spikes embedded in the bottom, lightly covered on top. A type of lethal trap.

Tourniquet: Last-resort treatment for serious bleeding (not controlled by direct or arterial pressure). Reduces circulation by constriction. (Must be carefully watched and released periodically to avoid profound tissue damage to the affected limb.)

Trail: The last shooter in a patrol formation and third in command of the fire team.

Traps: Potentially lethal pits or devices to protect a hardened residence.

Trigger finger management: Keeping the trigger finger outside the trigger guard unless a specific target is being engaged.

Trip wire: A thin dark wire that activates a signal or explosive device.

Unit standard: Standardized uniform and/or equipment to increase image of power and provide ease of sharing between fire team members.

Volume of fire: The capacity to deliver multiple rounds rapidly; varies based upon the nature of the weapon.

Voluntary compliance: Persuading looters to seek other targets without having to fire on them.

Wag: A rapid flat-hand up-and-down movement in front of the chest, signifies "I don't understand/agree."

Warming facility: A small tent that can be heated with a mini-stove or lantern to provide an area to warm dependents or team members.

Web gear: A combat harness that carries spare magazines, canteen, pistol holster, and personal med kit.

Wheeled cart: a.k.a gardeners cart, a large, man powered, open-topped cart for relocation of fire team gear or dependents.

INDEX

Acknowledgements

This book came to life because my son-in-law Chris and two of his closest friends, B.J. and T.J., took a serious look at preparedness and asked me to train them in team shooting. Between field-training events, I jotted down some thoughts on related issues, and before I knew it I was pushing two hundred pages. They are my "alpha team" and the baton could not have been passed to three finer young men. But no book is the author's alone, and this one especially is the product of other's creative and support efforts. My basic themes are only extensions of the thoughtful giants like Jeff Cooper, Mel Tappan, and Bill Jordan. If it were "dusted," lots of cop buddies have their fingerprints on this book; Dick and Steve, Bill, Bruce and Hal, Greg and Scott especially. Guys who proved that you can have a cool head and a hot gun behind you and always come out okay. A week under the nuanced coaching of Clint Smith at Thunder Ranch put a fine edge on the special weapons and tactics. My terrific editor at F+W books, Jackie Musser, was the perfect combination of firm hand and soft voice. Dr. James Hubbard was kind enough to review my medical chapter. And a special thanks to the sun around which my humble planet orbits … Kay.

About the Author

Joseph Terry is an experienced outdoorsman and retired police reserve sergeant with twenty-seven years on patrol and fifteen years as a member of his department firearms instructor's team. He has also published three books on organizational development and a memoir. Joe divides his time between homes and family in Northern California and Texas.

Disclaimer

This book is about desperate measures, justified only by desperate circumstances. Practicing the exercises in this book may cause serious injury or death. The use of "traps" and other anti-intrusion devices described in this book may cause serious injury or death. Unskilled persons providing medical care may cause serious injury or death. Certain recommendations in this book are prohibited by law and, if practiced, may subject the user to criminal prosecution. The author and publisher disclaim all responsibility for property damage, incarceration, injury, or death resulting from any person or persons acting on the recommendations, suggestions, training exercises, or combat techniques described in this book.

Other fine Living Ready books are available from your local bookstore and online suppliers. Visit our website at www.livingreadyonline.com. Living Ready® is a registered trademark of F+W Media.

18   17   16   15   14   5   4   3   2   1

ISBN 978-1-4403-3590-7

Distributed in the U.K. and Europe by F&W Media International, LTD
Brunel House, Forde Close, Newton Abbot, TQ12 4PU, UK
Tel: (+44) 1626 323200, Fax: (+44) 1626 323319
E-mail: enquiries@fwmedia.com

Distributed in Canada by Fraser Direct
100 Armstrong Avenue
Georgetown, Ontario, Canada L7G 5S4
Tel: (905) 877-4411
Distributed in Australia by Capricorn Link
P.O. Box 704, S. Windsor NSW, 2756 Australia
Tel: (02) 4560-1600
Fax: (02) 4577-5288
E-mail: books@capricornlink.com.au

Edited by Jacqueline Musser
Designed by Clare Finney
Production Coordinated by Debbie Thomas

BUG OUT BAG INVENTORY REVIEW SHEET

This five-page Bug Out Bag inventory Review Sheet will make packing and reviewing your Bug Out Bag's contents efficient and foolproof. Download it for free at **livingreadyonline.com/bug-out-bag-packing-list**

MORE BOOKS ON SURVIVAL AND PREPAREDNESS

Build the Perfect Bug Out Bag:
Your 72-Hour Disaster Survival Kit
by Creek Stewart

Living Ready Pocket Manual First Aid
by James Hubbard,
The Survival Doctor™

Food Storage for Self-Sufficiency
and Survival by Angela Paskett

AVAILABLE ONLINE AND IN BOOKSTORES EVERYWHERE!

Get free survival and preparedness tips! Join our mailing list at livingreadyonline.com.

Become a fan of our Facebook page: facebook.com/LivingReady